Let's Stop Tea
Start Designing Learning

M000277986

How can you shift from a focus on content to the creation of active learning experiences? In this practical resource, author Jason Kennedy provides a blueprint to help you stop "teaching" and start designing learning, so you can improve students' critical thinking, decision making, problem solving, and collaboration with others, preparing them for their futures beyond school doors. The framework for learning design covers components of planning (learning targets), of instruction (the opening, learning task, skills, tools, and success criteria), and of the work session (choices, pathways, feedback, and assessment). Appropriate for teachers of any subject area, the book also offers a wide variety of tools to help you implement the ideas in your own setting.

Jason Kennedy is a veteran educator, instructional coach, and school administrator who has over 22 years of experience at all levels of education.

Let's Stop Teaching and Start Designing Learning

A Practical Guide

Jason Kennedy

Routledge
Taylor & Francis Group

NEW YORK AND LONDON

Designed cover image: © Getty Images

First published 2023
by Routledge
605 Third Avenue, New York, NY 10158

and by Routledge
4 Park Square, Milton Park, Abingdon, Oxon, OX14 4RN

Routledge is an imprint of the Taylor & Francis Group, an informa business

© 2023 Jason Kennedy

Library of Congress Cataloging-in-Publication Data
Names: Kennedy, Jason, author.
Title: Let's stop teaching and start designing learning : a practical guide / Jason Kennedy.
Description: New York, NY : Routledge, 2023. | Series: Eye on education | Includes bibliographical references.
Identifiers: LCCN 2022054248 | ISBN 9781032431536 (hardback) | ISBN 9781032431277 (paperback) | ISBN 9781003365914 (ebook)
Subjects: LCSH: Active learning. | Instructional systems—Design.
Classification: LCC LB1027.23 .K46 2023 | DDC 371.3—dc23/eng/20230118
LC record available at https://lccn.loc.gov/2022054248

ISBN: 978-1-032-43153-6 (hbk)
ISBN: 978-1-032-43127-7 (pbk)
ISBN: 978-1-003-36591-4 (ebk)

DOI: 10.4324/9781003365914

Typeset in Palatino
by Apex CoVantage, LLC

Access the Support Material: www.routledge.com/9781032431277

To my family at home who love and believe in me, and to my family at every school who push me to do whatever it takes to make education better for staff and students.

Contents

About the Author

Jason Kennedy is a veteran educator, instructional coach and school administrator who has over 22 years of experience at all levels of education. As a college graduate with a degree in education, he entered the classroom challenged and energized in the teaching of his students. Now, he realizes that his job really was not supposed to be about his teaching, but about his students' learning. Now, his aim is to make learning the conversation around what happens in the classroom while providing teachers and leaders with tools to recalibrate the compass of education to its true purpose. Learning is the job, and it must be designed to be most effective.

Support Material

The tools from Chapter 8 of this book are also available on our website as free downloads so you can print them for your own use. To access the downloadable versions, you can go to the book's product page at www.routledge.com/9781032431277 and click on the link that says Support Material.

Introduction and Overview

First, My Apologies

Before I write anything at all, I want to say I am deeply sorry to all of the students I "taught" over the years. You may have enjoyed my classes, you may have learned some things, you may have even stopped me later at the grocery store or at the movies and told me how much you loved my class or shared some other compliment. Thank you for those words of praise; they kept me going through my years in the classroom. But looking back now, you deserved more. So please forgive me, former students. The only thing I can say about my teaching then is that I didn't know any better.

And the truth is, I really didn't. I went through my college education as a secondary education English major in the late 90s, and do you know how many education courses I had? Two. Neither one was about pedagogy or learning strategies or evidence-based practices to use in the classroom. Oh sure, I read about Piaget and Bloom and Maslow, but that was it. I did not have any formal education on how to actually "teach." Some would say, "Surely you had teaching observations and teaching practicum that prepared you." Yes, I did spend two weeks at the beginning of a school year observing one classroom, and a semester student teaching. But again, nothing really formally educated me on what learning was or how to

DOI: 10.4324/9781003365914-1

make it happen in a classroom. Luckily, the mentor teacher who supervised me during my student teaching was one of the most dynamic in the school. On day one, after observing her classes all day, we sat down together after the last bell in an empty classroom, and she looked at me and said, "So, what are you going to do tomorrow?" *GULP*. That was my initiation into education. Trial by fire to say the least. She turned me loose in her tenth-grade World Literature classes for the remainder of that fall semester, and by Christmas break, I was a state-certified educator.

I am so thankful for my supervising teacher, for her guidance and also for her trust in me to take her students from her for a semester and, for lack of a better word, experiment on them. I can't help but think about how many other educators there are in countless classrooms today who experienced the same type of preparation as a teacher. Or even worse, those who had even less. With the ever-evaporating pool of qualified teaching applicants, many school systems are turning to less experienced and even less credentialed educators to fill vacancies in the classroom. And this was happening long before a global pandemic pushed all educators to the brink, and many past that point. I cannot tell you how many regional education agency trainings I have attended, where I heard about the plight of other school systems with noncertified teachers leading their classrooms. All too often, those schools were the ones filled with students on the low end of the socioeconomic scale, and also the schools who needed great teachers the most.

I could spend the rest of this book citing all sorts of statistics or research on a lot of things related to the preparation of our teachers. I can point to the graphs and charts detailing all the correlations and effects on student achievement this type of educator neglect is having on our schools, communities, and economies. Throwing all the articles and academia at you, the reader, is the last thing I want to do with this book. What I would like to do with this book is provide something for the veteran teachers, like myself, to take in, reflect on, and rethink the way we've done things all these years.

To the Veterans

Alright veterans, we are probably the hardest ones to convince. We've been doing this teaching thing for a minute, and we think we have got it down. Some of us are stuck in our ways, using the old "tried and true" methods we have used for years now. Looking at what we continue to do though, have we ever stopped to think about whether or not what we are trying is *actually* true? Now before anyone gets offended, I hope you noticed I said "we" in this paragraph. I am guilty of some of the same deadly teaching sins that have killed some chances of some high-powered student learning taking place in some of my classes in the past. To some veterans, I will most definitely write some things in this book you will question, scrutinize, and flat out disagree with, and that's okay. If you take anything away from the pages to come, I hope it will at least cause a moment of reflection on our craft, challenge what we might see as true, or seek ways to improve instruction. Then again, maybe, you might just discover some new ways to improve learning in your classroom.

To the Newbies

I also want teachers new to the profession to step into a classroom with more knowledge and tools at their disposal in their first week of teaching than I did in my first ten years in the classroom. Those new to teaching, I welcome you to the hardest job there is, and possibly the most rewarding. As you probably have already realized about education, you will never have the same day twice. The thing I love most about new teachers is their willingness to be open to ideas and to collaborate with others. Some call that willingness, others call it desperation. Whatever you call it, keep it up for as long as you can. It will be one of the things that motivates you to grow in your professional knowledge and to hone your craft continually. My hope for you and this book is that it becomes a resource and base for you to build upon for the years you have ahead of you. Like I wrote earlier, I didn't know any better. No one taught me about learning and how I should best provide it to my students. Please take what is to follow, make it your own, and provide the greatest learning possible to your students you can. They are counting on you.

To the Leaders

Never wanting to leave our leaders out of the conversation, school leaders and administrators, perhaps this book will provide you a differently focused lens to use to look through when observing teachers and seeking to support them in the tremendous job that they do. You *have* to be a part of this conversation. As a school leader, I had these two questions on my desk to reflect on daily: "What did you do today to promote student learning?" and "What did you do today to support teachers?" That's the job in the simplest statement possible. Promote learning and support teachers. Everything else can wait, and should wait. Most of you leaders, perhaps, like many veterans and myself, were never really exposed to what learning takes or how it should look or what a teacher can do to make it happen in the classroom. We can pick out our strongest teachers in our buildings, we can notice engaging lessons at times, and we can even judge what quality work looks like from students. But leaders, how many of us can explain why our strong teachers are strong using the language of learning? Can we explain the importance of evidence-based strategies incorporated into lesson designs? Can we identify what we should be looking for in the classroom when observing students that shows they are actually learning or just faking it? Hopefully this book will provide some examples for you to use as well. Leaders and administrators, we should know what to look for from teachers in every part of a lesson. We should also know what to look for from students during their learning. And we should be able to support our teachers in designing learning as practitioners of the craft. We are leaders for others to *follow* after all, not in word, but in action. I want this book to be a guidebook for you as you observe the classrooms, lead your staff, and motivate the students.

What to Expect

So to wrap this up, I am really not writing anything that is all that new or cutting-edge revolutionizing education. You'll see references to research you may recognize like Hattie, Dufour, Marzano, and others sprinkled here and there. But my true mission for this book, my "why" for its publishing, is I want this book to be practical and real for those wanting to make learning the vision for the classroom. I want all the jargon and statistics that many of us trip over stripped away, and for us to get down to some common logic, beliefs, and reasoning behind why we should stop teaching and start to design learning.

For some, I hope this book provides a foundation of practical resources for you to use to create and design your own learning in your classroom. For others, this could help clarify what to look for in a classroom that shows learning, and not just teaching, is taking place. There will be some things among these pages you are familiar with, and you will say to yourself, "Oh, I knew that; I've *been* doing this." If you are responding with that, then take what you know and pass it on to those who don't. There will be some things you read that will cause you to pause, reflect, and stretch what you believe about what you do in the classroom. To that I say, there is nothing wrong with that at all! Our jobs require continually looking at what we do, why we do it, and if it is working.

Finally, there will be those readers who may take some of this personally and not be receptive to a lot of what I am sharing. To them, I make no apologies. Education is in an ever-changing, never-ending continuum of flux. We have to reflect and change with it and do whatever it takes. That may mean giving up that tried and true teaching, so that students can try even truer learning. Learning IS the job. It always has been. And we have to design for it.

Book Overview

Chapter 1: Why We Need to Stop Teaching
Chapter 2: Who Stops Teaching?

Chapter 3: Start Designing With the End
Chapter 4: The Opening
Chapter 5: The Work Session
Chapter 6: The Instruction
Chapter 7: The Close
Chapter 8: Tips, Tools, and Templates

1

Why We Need to Stop Teaching

Ms. Mitchell's Class

It was a typical Tuesday in Ms. Mitchell's classroom. The morning was filled with new concepts her students were learning. She spent some time presenting the new material and reviewing the upcoming student work. Ms. Mitchell was lively, engaging students with her positivity and humor. The children sat quietly, working on their assignment with the occasional hand raising to ask a question.

Ms. Mitchell was so excited about collecting the finished work and grading the assignment. She loved handing the graded work back out to students and seeing the delight on their faces or answering questions for those needing extra assistance. Her classroom was full of orderly students, who typically did all that was asked of them, filling her with a sense of accomplishment that they all were learning at their highest potential. There were those occasional moments when a student or two would succumb to other influences and slip off into conversations, daydreams, or other off-task behaviors. But, Ms. Mitchell handled those in stride. Teaching was her calling, and she knew the material learned today in class would be carried by her students as they left her classroom.

At the end of her day, looking out at the orderly rows of empty desks, Ms. Mitchell breathed a momentary sigh of satisfaction. Another day of school had come to a close, and it was one

DOI: 10.4324/9781003365914-2

she could be proud of knowing she fulfilled her teacherly duties. Ms. Mitchell gathered her things, preparing to leave. Closing her classroom door, she walked outside thankful that Mr. Langford from town had left his old mare for her to ride home instead of making the four-mile walk herself. The year was 1923.

Up until that last part with Ms. Mitchell having to use a horse for transportation home, you may have thought what was being described was any typical classroom from anywhere in the world last Tuesday. The point is, we have been teaching the same way for over a century now. However, we know now more than we ever have about learning, what impacts learning, and what can be purposefully designed into learning to improve what we do in the classroom. But still, the desks-in-rows, compliance-driven, traditional teaching model seems to predominate. Even with the pandemic, forcing a nation of schools into a variety of digital learning arenas, we still tended to keep on teaching the way it has always been done. I am just as guilty of teaching this way for years. The reason: No one ever taught me what it takes to make learning happen. I learned my content area in college and basically mimicked the most influential teachers I had growing up. So, now that we know better and know more, what will we do with that?

There's never been a better time to transition from teaching to learning as we move back into the classroom. Please don't take this as teacher bashing. Teaching is the hardest job there is. The reason I wrote this was for teachers, to help take some of the pressure and work off of them as we work through this thing we call public education. Does teaching work and has it worked? Sure, otherwise I am sure it would have been abandoned long ago. But, is teaching the way in which we have the best for everyone? There are a few innate flaws in the practice we can turn around for the benefit of both students and teachers alike. Our students deserve it; our teachers deserve it. Stopping teaching to design learning can benefit both.

Reason #1 to Stop Teaching: It's Passive

The most important reason why we need to stop teaching and start designing learning is that teaching, in general and traditionally, is passive. Students come to class, get information or have skills modeled for them, then they complete work. Repeat for next class. Basically, we could replace this same process with YouTube videos and save a lot of time and money.

I will give a shout-out to the elementary teachers out there. Out of the three levels of school – elementary, middle, and high – you all tend to lean more toward active learning rather than passive teaching. However, I have been in many elementary classrooms where the teacher "stands and delivers" while the students "sit and get" on a regular basis. Middle school and high school teachers, we are chief of sinners when it comes to this.

What's so wrong with the way we teach? The answer lies in that the passive nature of teaching typically leads to focusing on content and compliance over critical thinking and creativity. Some of you now are reading this and thinking, "Oh, he's one of *those* educators." Well, if you are implying that I believe that, in the words of John Keating from Dead Poet's Society, "the idea of education was to learn to think for yourself," then yes, I *am* proudly one of those educators. What our students need most out of teachers is not content knowledge, but active, critical learning experiences.

Think about it. Our public education system should be producing citizens who are ready for higher learning, technical training, or gainful employment. We prepare them for these destinations by having them sit in rows, listen to instructions, complete worksheets or answer questions, and turn in the results. Very little of that process involves critical thinking, decision making, collaboration with others, testing differing methods, tackling problems as they arise. Basically, everything that the real world will ask of them as adults and also what employers are begging for in future employees. The last time I checked, I had not seen a listing for "Worksheet Completer" on Indeed. If worksheets were created for learning, they'd be called "learning sheets." But where's our current focus? On the work instead of the learning, so worksheets live on.

The fact is that the act of teaching, the passive way we tend to do it now, can be a quickly and assumedly effective improvisation even rookie teachers can perform at a moment's notice.

I have been guilty of it; I've seen countless others do it as well. If you are looking for and at teaching, then there are many of us who seem to have "the teaching thing" down. I never want to say of myself again, "I am a great teacher," because that's not what this education thing is about.

Learning is what we are paid to provide, and that takes time and thought and purpose to design. It takes preparation, which most teachers have built into their workdays, to make the intentional choices in the information, skills, and tools required to provide to students so that they can demonstrate learning in an effective and visible way. You can "see" learning in a classroom where it has been designed around and for. It's there and in your face and you can talk with students in an active-learning classroom and they can tell you the answers to the three magic questions, "What am I learning?" "Why am I learning it?" and "How do I know I've learned it?"

But I can walk into a class where teaching is happening, and learning is hidden. You have to dig for it. It's inconsistent and rare because it was not designed or prepared for. Compliance is king. It looks good on the outside, desks in rows, quiet, work being completed, but where is the learning? After all, that is the reason why the school was built and the teachers were hired and the administration was put into place. Learning *is* the job, and we have to design for it.

Reason #2 to Stop Teaching: It's Not Engaging

Before anyone gets offended, let's reflect on the nature of teaching in the traditional sense. It often involves the delivery of information by a single individual. Only *one* person – whether it's the teacher or even a chosen student in class to read aloud, work a problem, or model a skill – is fully engaged. What is happening with the other 29 in the room? Can we know as teachers that the rest are engaged, attentive, and learning something? What and where is the evidence?

Think about this and think about engagement. Some classrooms have students enter. They complete a warm-up activity; the teacher may review it then give directions for work. The students then work, and turn that in by the end of class. Granted, there may be some notes or lectures mixed in between some of that, but this image of what is happening in thousands of classrooms every day of the week is some of our students' reality. Can we expect high levels of student engagement in environments like this? If we are honest and want engagement, the answer is "No."

The passive nature of teaching, as I mentioned, is the primary cause. Look, we teachers can sing, dance, stand on our heads, do the best John Keating/Robin Williams inspirational impression we can, but at the end of the day, *we* are the ones who are fully engaged. We are the ones talking, showing, working, moving, and being completely engaged in the information of the lesson. What about the students? How do we find and measure engagement?

We try to find it. Many of us stop and ask questions. But how many of us ask the same students most of the time to respond? Some of us ask students for a sign of attentiveness, like a head nod or a thumbs up, but does this really give us any tangible data to use in order to measure learning? So many of our students, and this is especially true in middle and high school, can easily hide every day in the classroom and do a great job at faking their learning. If I am a quiet and compliant student, who does my work without disrupting class, things will be fine. They sit and appear to listen, complete a worksheet or set of questions, and move on to the next day. Compliance is *not* learning.

A far worse side effect of teaching not being engaging is seen in those students who aren't compliant and fight their learning. They are most likely so bored with the same old work that they have no other recourse but to become a behavior problem. That only leads to even more issues, not only for the teacher trying to manage a classroom, but for the students who have been disengaged and unchallenged for years now not learning anything because what was being asked of them was only to sit, be quiet, and work. Work that did not seem relevant or much of a challenge in the slightest.

What's the solution? Stop teaching and start designing. Design the learning to include opportunities to collaborate, tasks that make learning visible, dialogues surrounding the material, and practices that promote mutual accountability to each other and not just the individual. Weston Kieschinck put it this way,

> Engagement is far too important to merely cross our fingers and hope teachers figure it out on their own. If history tells us anything, some will figure it out on their own, many won't, and others will try so hard to chase it that they'll run themselves right out of the profession.
>
> (2022)

Learning takes work ahead of time, especially when it comes to designing engaging learning. It takes preparation of tasks, attention to detail, consideration of pitfalls, and many other things. The great thing you get in return in the classroom is a lot less work on your part as the teacher because the learning has been handed over to those for whom it was meant for in the first place, the students.

Reason #3 to Stop Teaching: It Can *Cause* Misbehavior

I realize my first two reasons for teachers to stop teaching were student-centered in nature. Teaching is passive, and it is not engaging. So for this next reason, I felt I should give one with the classroom educator as the focus. For teachers, stopping teaching and designing learning will improve positive student behavior and cut out opportunities for misbehavior in your classrooms. Some might be thinking the next thing I will start presenting is some timeshare opportunity for you to invest in, but truly, hear me out. If we stop traditionally teaching and instead design for learning, students will cause less negative disruptions and you will not have to discipline nearly as often as you do now.

It points back to what's already been said, that teaching, by its nature, is passive and unengaging for students. What happens when you as an adult get bored with something you are doing or listening to or participating in as part of a group? Think back to the last professional development you might have attended. You began to doodle, get out your cell phone, open a tab on Pinterest, or start a conversation with a neighbor around you. Do any of these off-task behaviors sound familiar? They are present in a lot of school classrooms nationwide where teaching is taking place. Why?

It goes back to engagement. If we are not given opportunities to think, discover, solve, explore, and reason, our brains find other ways to do those things that may not involve learning about the solar system or how to solve two-step equations. Teachers have to design for learning by giving information out in shorter bursts along with intellectually engaging things for students' brains to be occupied by in order to fight off the misbehaviors brought on by boredom. If we, as adults, struggle with it 15 minutes into a presentation, why do we expect a 12-year-old to be able to be attentive and engaged in the same situation?

So, let's say you have kids who are engaged, finding the teaching challenging, or who are not easily bored. Then we must consider what lies on the other end of the instructional spectrum: the fact that some things we are asking of students are too much for their cognitive load to handle. Students see a daunting task and, whether by its difficulty or quantity, they tend to shut down. Again, when students shut down, there has to be a place for that energy to flow to, and that usually ends up being misbehavior.

This is where teachers, particularly in the middle and high school arena, have to find ways to design possibilities for student exploration, discovery, and reporting-out. Teachers are not the sole keepers of knowledge. Middle and high school teachers teach the way they do because it has been passed down that way. If all we are as teachers is a method of content delivery, then, again, we can be replaced today by YouTube. But, if a teacher chooses to be a "learning engineer," then that teacher designs for learning to happen in the room in ways clearly observed by all. Learning is a proactively planned event in which learning engineers craft every task, success criteria, formative checks, collaborative opportunities, and all the other components around.

There is a trade-off for becoming a learning engineer instead of a teacher. How many days do you leave, exhausted, while watching your kids do cartwheels out of the school doors? If you are willing to trade all the time you spend running from one student to the next in a classroom of 30 students, to trade the repeated redirection of behaviors and the constantly rising blood pressure you have trying to teach, then start designing learning. Marzano noted, "Misbehaviors. . . were so rare in the highly motivating, engaging classrooms that we leave this study still not certain what the consequential policies were in any of the. . . highly engaging classrooms" (2007). We can all have classrooms like this, if we design for them.

The trade-off is this: stopping teaching requires a lot of prep work, more than you have ever done before, but you will get all of your daily class time and physical energy back. You will not have to run around the room, redirect, correct, and manage a class of 30. Becoming a learning engineer will take many of the burdens you carry from bell to bell away, so that learning becomes the work of those to whom it truly belongs: the students. Teachers, please stop teaching to ease your burden of classroom management. You will gain all the time and energy back you had, and the ones who leave your room exhausted everyday will be your students instead of you.

Reason #4 to Stop Teaching: It Doesn't Prepare Students, Not Really

In order to understand this reason, we have to think more along the lines of the process of teaching itself is not preparing students for the future rather than the content knowledge. No one will argue that in order to learn fourth-grade math content, students must have been prepared by content from third-grade math classrooms. What I contend is that teaching is not preparing our students to be the thinking, collaborating, professional, communicative, critical problem solvers they will eventually need to be later on in life. "Traditional teaching," as I have described before, and which will be summarized shortly, does not typically grow and foster these attributes in our students.

Traditional Teaching

- Teacher is engaged
- Teacher provides instruction, notes, questions, and answers
- Teacher sets the pace
- Teacher monitors
- Teacher expends all the energy
- Students "sit and get"
- Students can "hide" in their learning
- Students receive whole-group instruction with surface feedback
- Students are passive
- Boredom and behaviors can occur
- Classroom is quiet
- Compliance-driven

Here's a general rundown of what happens now. Many elementary school teachers teach the way we've been teaching for the last century, stressing the necessity of making sure kids are completing their work, sitting quietly, and being "good students" in order to prepare them for middle school. Middle school gets a little more rigid in their compliance-driven, traditional teaching models, stressing that they are only getting the students ready for high school. High school classes, in a lot of cases, consist of a lot of notes, sit and get, and passive learning because that's what students will be experiencing when they get to college. And our higher institutions, well, they dump a vast amount of content-specific information, assess the retaining of that information, and turn graduates out into a workforce that they have not been prepared for in the slightest when it comes to many of the skills that really matter to the job in the first place.

What are those skills that are seldom addressed by traditional teaching? Apparently, they are the skills that have been sought after for over a century now. I found a study as far back as 1918 by C.R. Mann, entitled "A Study of Engineering Education," where the need for what we now call "soft skills" was noted as being just as important to the engineering profession as the technical knowledge students learn as part of the curriculum (Mann, 2016). Jumping ahead to this past year, in 2021, America Succeeds published "The High Demand for Durable Skills," detailing the need for skills in jobs from all sectors and that the "seven out of ten most requested skills" are not being addressed in our current classroom. According to their study, completed over two years and looking at over 82 million jobs, 52.5 million of those job postings asked for these "durable," "21st century," "human" skills. The skills that employers are begging for out of prospective employees are abilities in communication, interpersonal relationships, professionalism, quality decision making, reflective practices, teamwork, problem-solving, critical thinking, ethical behavior, flexibility, leadership, and diversity, just to name a few (Cole et al., 2021).

Traditional teaching practices may hit on some of these intermittently from time to time over the average course of a college education. However, it is surface-level at best. Designing active learning experiences that imbed opportunities for these skills to be constantly and continually developed is key to truly preparing our students for the actual reality they will face in the post-education workplace. Designing learning flips the traditional teaching classroom into one that looks a little different.

Designing Learning

- ◆ Students are engaged
- ◆ Students absorb, collaborate, and create around information and designed tasks
- ◆ Students set the pace
- ◆ Students monitor themselves and peers
- ◆ Students expend all the energy
- ◆ Students are mobile in learning
- ◆ Students monitor and explain learning
- ◆ Students talk more than the teacher about the learning
- ◆ Students are active
- ◆ Students are motivated and on task
- ◆ Classroom is noisy
- ◆ Learning-driven

I know of no job that consists of daily sitting at a single desk, quietly reading and responding to questions or completing a worksheet, which results in a paycheck at the end of the week. Yet, this is the reality we are preparing our students for? I wish someone would pay me my current salary to complete worksheets or answer those questions at the end of the reading selection. If you know of anyone hiring for that position, please send me the information, I'm interested.

Until those types of jobs become mainstream employment venues, we need to rethink what we offer to students in their learning. We need to design those opportunities for them to learn not only the "what" of the content we present them, but the "whys" and the "hows" as well. We must incorporate communication, teamwork, and self-assessment into what they do. They must be given chances to reflect, analyze their errors, and pass judgment on their own thinking. Students cannot learn how to be flexible and persevere through situations, how to utilize and evaluate tools in solving problems. I could go on, but these opportunities tend not to just "happen" in the classroom naturally when we teach. They result from intentional, learning-design choices.

We owe it to businesses to provide them with a ready and able workforce. We owe it to students, who spend almost two decades in an educational setting only to find they have a lot more to learn. We need to really prepare our students for what is really out there.

But, seriously, if you find out about that worksheet job, let me know.

Reason #5 to Stop Teaching: It Provides EQUALITY, But Not EQUITY

Bear with me through the following metaphor. Right now, students line up outside of classroom doors in a vertical line, one behind the other. Those in the front are much closer to the classroom door, much closer to the learning about to take place inside.

Now, while this random lineup of students happens in the literal world, figuratively speaking the students in the "front of the line" come into learning with a lot more advantages than those behind them. These students in front come with parental support at home, extra money for supplies, benefits from an exceptional teacher previously, and a number of other factors. They've been exposed to a lot more things that translate into more positive experiences in the classroom and in learning. These students are often the ones who get to see themselves and their families and backgrounds in the texts and materials offered in the classroom. These students toward the front of the learning line will have less difficulty when engaging with instruction, communicating needs, and many other actions involving their learning.

Those students toward the "back of the line" are entering learning facing a great divide in front of them. They may not have parents who are able to assist them at home. Their families were never able to afford additional supplies or resources. These students were not accelerated in their learning by a former teacher. These students have systemic barriers, erected generations ago, that need tearing down. These children enter the room far away from the front and may often face difficulty when learning.

Our job as educators is to transform this vertical line entering the classroom, where some students already have closer access to the learning while others have a longer distance to travel to get there, into a horizontal line where all students have equal access to the learning and mastery of the standards in our rooms.

You see, we've been providing equality for a while now: all students receiving the same treatment, materials, and instruction. Teaching, in the traditional and general sense, is often a "one-size-fits-all" delivery. This keeps that vertical line vertical. Those students with the preloaded advantages have much less farther to go to get to the learning today. Those in the back of the line struggle to close the wide gap they walked into the classroom with. These students are not low; these students have a farther distance to cover based on many things mostly out of their control.

Designing learning is the answer to making learning an equal reach for all students. Purposeful, instructional design will allow for the tools for misunderstanding to be in place, for tasks to be intentionally created with students at all places in the vertical line in mind, for acceleration pathways to be laid out for students wanting to go deeper in their learning. Designing learning takes the line they entered class in and swings it around, allowing all students to have the same access in reaching the learning goals of the lesson.

The big surprise of it all is that designing learning really isn't *more* work, as many often assume or fear. Designing learning is just a little *different* work for the average teacher. It's about shifting the focus of what we get paid to do (which, again, is not teaching, by the way). It is providing learning. Learning that is rigorous for all with high expectations for all, relative for all with connections to their lives, and lastly, relational for all with evidence students can "see" themselves in the things they learn in school.

Right now, our students are lining up at our doors of learning in an order that is beyond their control outside of our classrooms. The second they enter, we must have learning designed and ready so that all can equally access it. This is the nature of education. It should be the great equalizer, and it is up to us as educators to do what it takes to provide this equity for our students. That means sometimes abandoning the "tried and true" because the way things have always been done is not working to level the playing field. Our students deserve no less from us. Design learning to give them the best and most equitable learning possible.

The Reward for Stopping Teaching to Start Designing Learning

Now you've read the reasons why we should stop teaching like we have been for the better part of a century. The question that might remain is, "What's the catch?" There really isn't one other than this: designing learning is about making the most effective and impactful choices for students' learning before you ever walk in the room. Some may say, "I do that already. I use my planning time and write lesson plans." Boy, there's an element of education we all have grown to love, lesson plans. I have written my fair share of those as well. But, designing is somewhat different.

Think about the words "plan" and "design." What's the difference? I always posed this question to teachers I worked with, "Who would you hire just based on the title itself for your next adventure, a vacation planner or a vacation designer?" You can interchange any major event noun in front of those words like "event," "wedding," or "birthday," and you'd get the same results. Everyone always picks *designer*. Why? To plan something is to arrange the parts of it somehow. Sounds a lot like an order or place type of focus. But, to design something is to devise for a specific function or end. I'd much rather go on a vacation that was designed for me, rather than just planned.

That's what design is all about, making those choices in every detail of what we do for the specific function and end of learning. And there are benefits for students and teachers, alike! Here's a brief list of those I've witnessed in my own classrooms and in the classrooms of others when you make designing for learning, instead of teaching the content, *the* priority.

Design-Learning Benefits for Students

1. *Students are engaged*. Engagement is not entertainment. It is the interest we construct through many of the chosen qualities we will put into learning. More on this later.
2. *Students will grow and gain higher achievement levels*. Obviously, when engagement happens, this often follows naturally. But, it also is a result of what has been designed for the students to show these levels of high learning.
3. *Students develop "soft skills."* These are the abilities so much of life (along with future employers) demand out of our students. Designing learning opportunities with these experiences embedded into them will result in world-ready students.

4. *Students will leave tired at the end of the day.* This probably belongs on the following list. Students will be the ones putting forth all the effort in their learning when we design for it.

Design-Learning Benefits for Teachers

1. *Teachers will see learning and experience success.* Right now, so many students hide in learning while others are not making the progress teachers desire. Designing learning will make the learning visible, thus allowing teachers to feel like they are gaining ground.
2. *Teachers will have more time and energy in class.* Whose learning is it after all? A design that hands learning over to students while a teacher facilitates will free up a lot of time and energy on the adult's part.
3. *Teachers will have less discipline issues.* Note, I did not say zero. If that were true, I would be obscenely rich. But, you will experience less because students' focus and energy will be reigned in through what you've designed for them to accomplish.
4. *Teachers will feel supported, happier, and willing to remain in the profession.* This is the hardest job there is. Designing successful learning will leave you feeling elated at the results, especially when you collaborate with your peers and share in the experience.

What Now?

If after reading you see what education has been (teaching) and what it could be (learning), you have made probably the most difficult part of the journey. Stopping teaching is more of a mindset and perspective change than anything else. Yes, there are things that are purely active-learning-driven that you will need to investigate, experiment with, and learn, but the most challenging part I have found for most educators is taking the initial steps to want to improve what we do in the classroom by stopping to teach.

Those initial steps often involve looking at education a little differently than we have been used to for the better part of the last century. Often before we can take on any new challenge, we first have to prepare ourselves. A lot of that work involves examining our thoughts and beliefs since our thoughts shape our feelings and our feelings influence our actions. Therefore, if we really want to accomplish something, it may take some reflection on what we've previously held as true while also being open to new ideas. The next chapter will narrow down some beliefs and attitudes necessary to make the work of designing learning much easier and effective for you as an educator.

Questions to Consider

1. Thinking back to your time attending school as a student, do you think what students experience in learning in the classroom of today is completely different or generally the same as your past education? Why? What looks the same? What looks different?
2. If you could change one thing about the traditional teaching occurring in classrooms over the last century or more, what would it be? Why?
3. What reason for stopping traditional teaching from this chapter grabbed your attention the most? Why this one?
4. Which reason do you feel has the most appeal to you as an educator? Which reason would have the most appeal to a student?
5. What is one thing you hope to gain by reading the rest of this book? Why?

Reference List

Cole, L., Cowart, C., Muller, S., & Short, S. (2021). *The high demand for durable skills.* https://americasucceeds.org/wp-content/uploads/

2021/04/AmericaSucceeds-DurableSkills-NationalFact Sheet-2021.pdf

Kieschinick, W. (2022). *The educator's atlas: Your roadmap to engagement.* ConnectEDD.

Mann, C. R. I. (2016). *A study of engineering education.* Creative Media Partners, LLC.

Marzano, R. J. (2007). *The art and science of teaching.* ASCD.

2

What Does Stopping Teaching Require?

More About a Mind Shift Than a Method

Again, the secret to this whole stopping-teaching-to-design-learning thing really is about a mind shift. It's a belief, a vision, an internal compass that you have to set to point toward learning. I don't know how old you are, reader. But I can remember a time when I saw this large, black, spinning sphere that was stuck to the dashboard of my grandfather's truck. I would watch it as we traveled, floating in that clear liquid, always pointing north. Inside of us, there's a compass. Something that points us in the direction of our choices and attitudes about our work. We have to choose to set our course toward learning. When that compass is set on learning and what it takes for your students to learn, all the things you think about, research, incorporate, strive for, and, most importantly, design everything around should point towards that goal. To stop teaching, you must use that compass to make intentional, purposefully impact-filled choices on every single thing we bring into the classroom for students, from what we spend our time on to what texts we read.

With that said, if we can agree that we all want students to learn and that we all want to do our very best at being successful in making learning happen for students, let's discuss some additional internal commitments you might want to adopt to make

DOI: 10.4324/9781003365914-3

the shift from teaching to designing learning. These attitudes, attributes, and beliefs are all prerequisites to making the job of becoming a learning engineer, who designs highly effective learning, a much easier job than that of the ordinary teacher. If we want all those benefits of designing learning discussed in the first chapter for our students and for ourselves, we first have to lay the internal groundwork on which to start.

What's Needed for Teachers to Stop Teaching

You Have to Love Students

Relationships are paramount. They drive everything we do, and not just at school. Our relationships with others are the only way we really get our work, goals, or dreams accomplished. Seldom is there anything we ever get done truly on our own. We always need others, and relationships are the lifeblood in working with others.

It is no different in the classroom. We have learning to accomplish in our students. That first involves establishing positive relationships with them. Before I say anything else, I have to say this. If you do not love kids, ALL kids no matter the gender, race, age, and any other identifier, then you are probably in the wrong profession. Love is a choice, sometimes a hard one. Don't get "love" and "like" mixed up here. I love my own children. I choose that daily. But there's been plenty of times I have not liked them. My academic kids are no different than my genetic kids. I choose to love them, even though there are days they can be very hard to like.

What does loving our kids mean for teachers? It means making the choices necessary each and every day in our words, actions, and attitudes towards our students to show them that no matter what happens, we care. This choice to love through our interactions with students requires us to be constantly mindful of so many things. We have to realize that inside this school and classroom may be the only time in our students' day where they will not be screamed at, much less hear anything positive from any adult. We have to realize they may have been up all night, arrived at school in dirty clothes, will be eating the only meals they will have today at school, and walk our halls weighed down with so many things, most of which are out of their control. We have to realize that when our students are having those "not-so-likable" moments, that is when they need us to love them the most. We have to know that we cannot take their actions and attitudes personally at times because the reasons behind their misbehavior in our rooms would most likely make us sad than make us angry.

Am I condoning a disorderly classroom where learning cannot take place? Of course not. What I am saying is we are in the learning business in education. When our kids show up to us not knowing how to add, subtract, or do long division, what do we do? We teach them. When they arrive in class not being able to write a coherent sentence or paragraph? We teach them. When students cannot explain the water cycle, or the property of waves, or photosynthesis? We teach them. Most of that learning is taught not by throwing a book at them, sitting them down to do an assignment, or telling them to figure it out on their own. We show them the expectation and model the actions. Yet, when a student does not display the "correct" behaviors in a classroom, the go-to is punishment, not learning. We should be modeling the learning of positive behaviors just as much as we do anything else we are trying to teach our students.

Remember this. We have to touch their hearts before we can ever try to put anything into their heads. Some may think this overly sentimental, but research tells us this works. While I will give the Cliffs Notes version in a few more pages, just trust me that the following numbers represent practices and influences that have a high potential impact on student learning. The impact of students feeling a connectedness to school has an effect size totaling 0.40. A positive student-teacher relationship has an effect size of 0.47. Teacher credibility has a 1.09 effect size (Corwin, 2021). All of these are elements we must take into account when we are choosing how to interact with our students and build those needed relationships. We *want* kids on our team. We *need* them on our team in this thing we are calling education. I would go into ways to do this, but that is a whole other book entirely.

But, at the core, remember they are children, expect them to act like the children they are and show grace when that happens. Trust me, if you have more relationships to foster with students than rules to follow, classroom behavior won't be an issue.

You Must Believe All Students Can Learn and Want to Learn

After choosing to love your students, even when it's difficult to like them, educators have to believe in them. The belief we need to hold onto as the base for everything else we do with them is this: "All my students can learn at the high standard I set for them." Notice, the word is ALL. All means all after all. The instant we think "These kids can't. . ." or "These kids won't. . ." you have already set the bar lower and expect less out of "these" kids just because of where they come from, where they live, who their parents are, how they behave, or any other criteria one can construct to make excuses around. The truth is these kids will *never*. . . if that's what the adults in the building believe about them. And that is on *us*.

You might be thinking, "You don't have the kids I have." You are right. But I have been in a school system who served a population that had the highest percentage of federal housing per capita in my state. I have had students from all types of households and from all kinds of backgrounds. Do some of our kids come to us with more exposure to things than others? Absolutely. Is it our job to meet kids where they are, provide the tools and scaffolding necessary to attain equity so all students have the same access to a high-quality curriculum and deeper learning experiences at the same high expectations? An even more emphatic absolutely!

I remember one year teaching eighth-grade English language arts. The class size started out at 27. Six of the students were identified as gifted, four were identified as special education students, and the remaining 17 were anywhere in between. Around three months into the school year, I received a new student. I will call him Mark. Mark was 13 years old. He had grown up chained to a bed, abused in every way, fed very little. Mark would yell out for attention or in anger. Mark would struggle. Mark would stand up randomly. Mark would shut down. Mark would eat food he had hoarded away in his backpack. But, with all the behavior challenges Mark brought in addition to the deficits in learning he entered my room with, I believed and expected him to learn. Did Mark require more one-on-one time? Sure. Did he, along with other students at different times, need some scaffolds and customized tools to build and coach him up to the level or performance I expected in their learning? Of course. My gifted, special education students, Mark, and everyone else all had to meet the same targets. I didn't move the finish line up for anyone. What I did do was provide ways to meet them where they were, design methods for them to access the learning with equity, and hold them all to the goal.

We cannot point at the students, point at their abilities, point at their home life, point at their poverty, point at their trauma, or point at anything else and lay the blame of a lack of learning. We do not teach labels; we teach learners. It is our job to design, collaborate, create, lift, intervene, scaffold, support, build, and everything else we can to make high levels of learning a reachable reality for those we often write off with a label. Labels or learners? Which will you teach? There is a right answer, not right as in "correct," but right as in just. We have to do the right thing for all students, and that begins with believing in all students.

You Must Know That Learning Is the Job and Do the Job of Learning

Learning IS the job. I really can't put it more plainly than that. The job isn't lesson plans, the job isn't classroom management, the job isn't teaching content. The job is learning. It is designing learning for our students while also being active learners in our own right. The second the adults in schools stop learning, that is the very same second all the students stop as well. We are in a profession after all, aren't we? We have college degrees, certifications, endorsements, and credentials. We have to learn ourselves and keep on learning if we are to be effective in designing learning for others.

If we truly buy into the fact that learning is indeed the job we sign up for, then there are two things we have to commit to do. First, we have to commit to the practice of everything we choose to implement having learning as its goal. I mentioned this earlier, and I know teachers already are overworked, under-appreciated, under duress and overloaded. But, we have to make a promise to do anything and everything for the sake of learning. Most of the time, that promise brings us face to face with a hard question.

I'm a movie fan. I'll watch just about anything, and usually more than once, much to the dismay of my wife. It's the English major in me, I guess, always looking at and studying stories, and how others choose to tell them in text or on film. One I can relate to here is a classic, *The Untouchables*. Kevin Costner, Robert De Niro, Andy Garcia, and of course the legend Sean Connery, whose character I'll be referring to here. The movie centers around Eliot Ness and his crew of agents taking on the infamous Al Capone during Prohibition. In my favorite scene in the movie, Sean Connery's character, Jim Malone, meets his demise at the hands of one of Capone's lackeys. Costner plays Eliot Ness, arriving just a little too late to save his fellow agent and friend. Following a bloody trail left by Malone dragging himself through his apartment, Ness kneels at the side of his dying friend. Malone gives Ness the location of what will eventually be the person who puts Capone away. His dying words to Ness are these, "What are you prepared to do?"

That's how I feel about the learning we provide for our students. I feel like we should wake up, walk into the schoolhouse, look ourselves in the mirror, and ask, "What *are* we prepared to do?" Do teachers do too much as it is? Of course. But we are also pouring in a whole lot of time, energy, and ourselves into practices and resources that are not all that meaningful (if at all) to student learning. We need to be prepared to do whatever it takes for learning to be accomplished. The last line Kevin Costner as Eliot Ness says in the movie is directed at Al Capone, in an explosive courthouse where Capone is being tried for tax evasion. Ness says, "Never stop fighting till the fight is done. . . . Here endeth the lesson."

Our fight is ongoing, and it does not end until one of two things happen. First, the fight ends when every student is displaying learning at high and appropriate levels. Or, the fight ends when we give up on finding ways to reach students who some adults have labeled as unable to reach or "untouchable," and provide them with whatever they need for their learning.

That is the job. Learning. Every. Student. Learns. That takes dedication. It requires design, intent, and purpose. Learning IS the job. What are you prepared to do?

You Must Know Your Choices for Learning Matter and See the Difference They Are Making

Now, this is one I missed out on in college, earning my degrees. It would be safe to say that if you have been in education for longer than ten years, you probably missed out on it as well. Like I mentioned in the introduction, most of my college courses were centered on content. Most middle and high school education degrees have that in common. Very content-heavy, pedagogically light. In the primary and elementary teaching degrees, most of the courses are heavily reading-instruction-based, skimming surface-level-content subject matter, combined with a few more courses centered on teaching, but still, the methods of teaching we've been doing the same way for over a century. It has only been during the last 15 years or so that educational research has begun to focus on the science and qualities that promote, inspire, create, manifest, or any other word meaning "make" learning happen in the classroom.

So, what do we know now that we didn't know then that makes this whole "stop teaching to design learning" thing matter to what I do in the classroom? This is where things get all scientific and research-heavy for a bit. Here's the shorthand version of the effect-size research published by John Hattie and Gregory Yates in *Visible Learning* in 2009. Basically, an effect size is a statistical number that represents how well or poorly something works at changing an outcome. In other words, let's say you wanted to lose ten pounds. Eating lettuce on a consistent and regular basis to lose said pounds would have a greater effect size than eating ice cream would. Sounds like common sense, right? Some things work better than others at gaining certain outcomes.

How does this apply to education? In *Visible Learning* (2009), Hattie and Yates gathered information into what is called a "meta-analysis," meaning basically they collected all the educational research and studies from all over, compiled the data together, found themes and patterns, and what resulted was a list of just about anything having any kind of possible impact on students' learning. This collection of studies involved hundreds of thousands of studies and hundreds of millions of students. As a result, we now have a list of 320 factors that have some type of influence (positive or negative) on student learning. Educators can examine these when making choices that involve the things we have control over like teaching strategies, curriculum, classroom dynamic, technology, and many of the other aspects we have to decide on when designing learning.

How do we use this information to design learning? We have to keep in mind a specific number. That number is 0.40. This is the number that represents one year's worth of input resulting in one year's worth of growth. In other words, if a student comes to school for a year and just "does school," we can expect the result to be 0.40 for the effect size. Any method, strategy, tool, treatment, intervention that has an effect size *lower* than 0.40 has less of an impact than just attending during a typical school year would have. Those are probably things we do not want to keep in our practices since they are not really making a difference. Even more shocking, there are things involving students that have a negative effect size, meaning that these may cause our students to regress.

What we need to make common practice is making choices in what we provide our students in learning that contains the most impact potential. Anything over 0.40 effect size has the potential in growing students as much as, if not more than, a year's worth of schooling. Looking back at the examples I cited previously, Teacher Credibility (students being able to trust that a teacher is competent enough and cares enough to learn from) has a 1.09 effect size (Corwin, August 2021). If we equate a year's growth with 0.40, then this influence has the potential of two and a half years' worth of growth. Jigsaw, a popular instructional strategy, has an effect size of 1.20 (Corwin, August 2021). Does that mean that if I Jigsaw with my students next week, they will grow three years in their learning? Of course not. But there are things we must consider and put into practice that do make these effect sizes matter as meaningful to the learning in your classroom.

There are three key components in making these purposeful design choices centering on impacting learning:

1. Choose the influences with the *highest impact* and effect sizes that you can control in your room. It's your room, your lessons, your students; you know what works and what doesn't. Also, look at any current practices with a low impact. Are they worth the time and energy placed into them if the outcomes for learning aren't as high as we would like?

2. Use these high-impact practices *often, well,* and *long-term.* These criteria must be followed if we want to see the results of our impact. Often: these are components we purposefully incorporate in our lessons as much as possible. Well: we implement these at the highest level of quality possible. Duration: we continue to make these components part of our practice all school-year long.

3. Examine the results to *see* the growth. Part of Collective Teacher Efficacy (effect size = 1.36) is that teachers not only believe they are making a difference and put the practices in place to make that difference, they also can point to the results with confidence saying, "See, we know it's working because . . ." (Corwin, August 2021).

If we want to become learning engineers and design the highest quality learning, we have to make intentional, purposeful decisions in those designs using the science to back up our choices, and turn around to see and celebrate the successes in our students' learning. You'll see more on impact and effect sizes as we move ahead together. Just know that what you choose has impact.

You Must Value and Seek Out Collaboration

We can't do this job alone. I will say that again. We cannot do this job all on our own. Why would you want to? Still, there are some teachers who want to remain in their rooms, close their doors, and worry about their classrooms only. Middle and high school teachers, we are the ones who typically have the hardest time with this one. After all these years being in middle and high schools, I still haven't figured out why.

It might be a scheduling thing. It might be a cultural thing. It might be a "we've never seen what collaboration can do for us" kind of thing. In any case, there's so much to be gained from collaborating with our peers in this work we do. There are so many benefits true collaboration in schools for the mission of learning can bring to teachers. One of my favorite quotes about teacher collaboration is this: "It is difficult to overstate the importance of collaborative teams in the improvement process. It is even more important, however, to emphasize that collaboration does not lead to improved results unless people are focused on the right work" (DuFour et al., 2016). The right work is all about our students' learning.

Collaboration allows us to share the workload. Whether your school is involved in Professional Learning Communities (PLCs), you plan with some fellow teachers down the hall, or you are a singleton at your school with no one else teaching like content, you can find avenues to collaborate with fellow educators and share this workload we bear. "Another universal truth in education is that it is virtually impossible for individual teachers to possess all the expertise and resources needed to address the variety of student needs in their classrooms" (DuFour et al., 2021). We have to make collaboration a priority if we want to do what is best for the students in our rooms. It will improve your practice, provide you with a resource like no other, and promote a culture you will never want to be without again.

For you PLC practitioners and teachers with peers in the building, start coming together and work with a collective purpose. These meetings aren't just another meeting and they should never be about filling out a form or checking a box. We come to collaborate in order to improve learning for our students. We come together to help one another in answering those questions that DuFour and others (2016) helped identify that show what our work really is all about: 1. What do we want kids to learn? 2. How will we know they've learned it? 3. What will we do for kids who didn't meet the learning expectation? 4. What will we do for those who did? Sometimes those are hard questions to tackle, especially when we try to do it on our own. That is why we need each other. That is why we collaborate. All the expertise, skill, and knowledge exists in the walls of our schools already. We know the content, we know what it should look like, we know how to help those who aren't quite there yet, and we know how to make paths to go beyond. The more of us working together in the process, the more ideas, strategies, lessons, activities, and experience are brought to the table for all of us to share and make our own individual classrooms better. Why would we ever want to do all this work alone?

For you singletons, technology has never been more ready to help you in connecting with others like you. We have so many tools at the ready, in our own pockets even, to be able to video conference, share documents, work out ideas in real time from the other side of the country if need be, that it's almost like working with someone down the hallway. We have neighboring districts that surround us, or even those within our state we can find ways to link with to improve learning. At the very least, a singleton can find a community on social media to interact with and have some of the same discussions, share some of the same resources, and make decisions benefitting the learning of students.

I would wager that there is enough talent, knowledge, and expertise in the building you work in currently, that if the adults in the school would come together, place real value on collaboration, put shared beliefs and values in place in regards to what we are supposed to do for students, and make it a culture to meet, collaborate, and do what's best for kids on a regular basis, that there is no limit to the achievement you will see from your learners, and it will not cost you a penny in professional development nor will it require any more hours outside of what you are already working. Looking back at that sentence, I see that was a *lot*. But what it says is also true. Value, believe, use, and improve collaboration, and teachers, you will find success.

What's Needed to Instill in Our Learners

You know, teachers are not the only ones in the classroom. We are outnumbered, and we know it. We have this mass group we are charged to interact with, instill learning in, and yet, sometimes we are so focused on the content that we miss the cognition. We worry about the lesson, but what about the learning? How can we move to a classroom culture orbiting around the purpose we all are here for? We do that by letting the big secret out to the kids: that you are not coming to school to remember facts, mimic skills, or "do work." You are here to learn, and learning isn't about textbooks and tests; it's about a practice and a process that you need to know all about. What if we filled our kids in on what learning is and what it requires?

Students Need to Know What Learning Is Before Their Lessons

Imagine what would happen if we spent the first week or so of each school year embedding what learning is and what learning requires into our school-wide beliefs and expectations *with* our students. What I mean is, before we ever opened the first notebook, assigned the first reading or gave the first math problem, what if we got our students to understand the process of learning, the passion it requires, the progression it involves, the pitfalls they will face, and the promise that lies at the end of it all?

I'm not talking about the rituals and routines of compliance. We continue to drill those into our students from day one. Students know they need to sit, do their work, raise their hands, and all the other procedural aspects. Is there a need for that? Yes. But do we ever stop and prepare them for the actual learning process with as much intensity and fervor as we do these compliance-centered protocols? What if we spent the same time and energy on sharing with students that learning is a process that is backed by evidence-based research, or that an activating strategy is designed to bring your prior knowledge up to help you think about today's learning? What if students knew there will be times they will face something they can't figure out, and that working through that was a natural part of learning? What if they knew all the aspects of learning, could talk about learning just as we talk about any other content-based subject in class, and saw the big picture in what we, as the teachers, are designing for them? Imagine the possibilities.

How could we get this accomplished? Even if it wasn't a school-wide cultural commitment, a single teacher could take the time to, along with routines, collaborate with students and establish some "What learning is" type of values and beliefs with students. Using these values and beliefs, form expectations of what learners do in your room that are not compliance- or procedure-based, but based on what learning is, what it requires mentally, what it requires emotionally, and anything else required on the part of the student to be successful in their learning with you. Make it the culture of your room, chant it, celebrate it. I guarantee results and that soon other classrooms will follow.

Students Need to Know It's Their Learning

Something else that we need to instill in our students as they enter our classrooms is this: everything we do here revolves around their learning. The instruction, the discussions, the devices, the materials, the desks, the texts, everything in this room is about and is used for learning. And the most important thing to get across to our students about this learning is that it belongs to them. Students are here to participate in that process, not as passive receptacles, but as active achievers. Ownership in learning, and what that looks like, is something we have to offer to our students, guide them through, and expect more of when we are together in class. It's their learning after all.

How do we get students to take ownership over their own learning? It's not about completing work or being responsible or displaying all those compliance-driven aspects we often associate with a "good student." Giving students ownership starts with allowing them to be a part of the process. It is about filling them in on all the things that adults talk about while sitting in meetings or the stuff that parents read about when certain reports are sent home. We need to share with students all the information we collect and have about them. Students should be given any type of achievement data and made aware of what this data means to their learning. Whether it's a standardized test, reading-level inventory, math fluency assessment measure, or any other data puzzle piece that the adults use to put together to form an academic picture of what a student knows and what the next steps will be, the students should be able to talk about it with their parents, with their teachers, with their peers, or anyone else they choose and how this information will help them in their learning.

For example, my students would conduct student-led conferences twice during the school year. This process involved the students collecting all sorts of artifacts concerning their learning, from an assignment in ELA that they did really well on to a math quiz that demonstrated the opposite. Students also collected information about their behavior, interests in school, and also interests outside of the classroom. They used all of this information, wrote a script to guide them along, and invited an adult to their conference in my room. I would have four or five of these going on at once, rotating out every 15 minutes or so. Standing at the door, I would greet the adults, invite the student to escort them to an open table, and my part was over. Students took the reins from there. Students would lead the discussion with their invited adults, review the artifacts they had collected as I monitored from the doorway. Along with the student-work examples they collected as artifacts, they were also required to review any data tied to their academic life at school. This could be last year's state-standardized-testing data or their current Lexile reading level. Students were aware of what all of their scores were, what each one meant, and were able to explain that to their invitees. Most important to this process, students set goals for their learning based on data, formulated steps they could take in order to meet these goals, and shared specific things the adults invited to the conference could do to also assist in meeting these goals as well. There was nothing else that ever came close to building a learning team with our students, the adults at home, and teachers at school than did this practice. Why? Because we turned the learning back over to whom it had always belonged.

But, it's not only about making students aware that school is about *their* learning. We also need students to understand that all of this is about their *learning*. All too often as students grow older, they enter into a mindset that education is a transactional process revolving around the work they complete and the grades they receive in return. That is *not* what school should be about. Education is about learning, and it's the reason they come to school in the first place. It is our expectations for them, and we need to make them a part of the expectation process as well when it comes to their learning.

I used to have expectations in my classroom, much like any other teacher. However, they were not called "rules," and they were not written by me. At the start of the year, my class and I discussed what learning is, what it involves, what it looks like, and all the rest. We all agreed the learning we would be participating in would be valuable and worth protecting. Together, we would write simple, shared commitments and place them in the room. There was a list of commitments and expectations the students wrote and chose to hold themselves and others accountable to throughout the year. There was also a list students made detailing what they expected of me during our time together. We all came together knowing that learning was the reason we were here and promised to do our best at seeing this through together.

Students Need to Realize Learning Is Hard Work

Let's be honest. Learning is hard. It takes time, concentration, perseverance, vulnerability, energy, and a whole lot of other things we don't even realize when we are in it. So, once we've made students aware of what learning is and that it's their learning, we have to find a way to get across the fact that learning will be difficult and will require students to "work for it." This type of work is not the typical work we see taking place in most classrooms. Students realizing the hard work of learning is mostly an internal exercise allows them to clearly see that learning work is much different than traditional school work.

The hard work of learning is one mostly consisting of students becoming aware of their learning surroundings, making intentional, internal choices of reactions, and realizing the results. When students first enter an area of new learning, they are anxious. We all are at some level whenever we are learning something new. There is an underlying nervousness, no matter how faint, that greets us when we set out to tackle a new concept or skill, no matter who's in the room. Students often face this anxiety in a room full of peers, which is obviously much more nerve-racking than me learning how to play the guitar by watching YouTube videos. In both cases, there is some level of angst, whether it's a third grader nervous about learning to multiply numbers in front of others or my being worried I just wasted several hundred dollars on a guitar I will never be able to play. So, what do we do? We have to let our students know that taking risks, being nervous, and feeling hesitant is part of learning. It always is and always will be. What they need to know most about confronting this feeling is that they are safe to take the risks in your room. They need to know being nervous is part of the adventure. Adventures require risk, curiosity, exploration, questioning, and most importantly, discovery. Learning adventures are no different.

Once students get over that brief initial bout with butterflies, it's time to address probably the hardest work about their learning during this process: their choices. There's so much going on in the room, at home, inside their heads, and with all that simulus, choices will arise. The results of these choices will either help students in their learning journey or sideline them. We have to help students recognize the things that sideline them in their learning, and that once they recognize the signs, they must make the best choices for their learning. When something draws their attention away, students need to know how to pull themselves back into learning. When facing a difficult task, students need to know how to push through with the methods you provide them. When they get stuck, students need to seek out ways to think around obstacles in the way of the goal. These actions, and so many others, are internal struggles as part of the work of learning that we seldom ever take students through, talk about, seek solutions for in order to really show our kids what the work of learning requires.

Students were in the thick of it, made their choices, worked through the muck and the mire in their minds, and came out the other side. The learning work is over, right? Not quite. Students also need to be shown the potential power in the pondering pause at the end of the process. In other words, they need to stop, look back at what just happened, find the value in it, and take away something with them for the next learning journey.

Sometimes, students will see that a brief moment of mindfulness when struggling through that math problem really helped out. Others might see that trying a different approach to what they were trying to do worked great. Still more may have realized that communicating their needs with others and collaborating made the hard work a little easier. Even when we think the learning is over, looking back always provides more lessons. Let's make sure the lesson that sinks in the most is that learning is not just a physically demanding job, but one that requires students to constantly be aware of the thinking and emotional work involved as well.

Students Need to Expect They Will Make Mistakes, and We Will Celebrate Together

If there was a metaphor for what I just described in the previous section, there is no better one than this: the hard work of learning is like playing a video game. Now, if given the time, I could probably apply the comparison to just about every type of video game that exists, but for the sake of brevity, I will just pick a tried and true, classic arcade scroller, *Super Mario Bros.*

Think about it. Back when it was first released in 1985, this video game was nothing like anyone had seen before. To make matters worse, there were no "level guides" or "walk-thrus" available for players back then. We stepped into a new and unfamiliar world and had to become aware of our surroundings. Players had to step out in this environment full of new experiences and suffer the real possibility of losing a life if we were not constantly being aware of what was going on around us. We had to focus, use trial and error, sometimes collaborate by handing off the controller to an older sibling to get us past a level or two. We had to figure out ways around, over, and under things. We made countless choices in all of this, resulting in sliding down that flagpole or rescuing the princess, after which we then could look back on and see what worked, what didn't, and what we might use next time to get a faster time or higher score. Now, I kept this analogy brief to make the connection that video games and learning both require similar types of hard work, but they also have one other quality in common: mistakes.

I can't tell you how many times Mario died, throwing his hands up in the air while flying upward and falling back down, disappearing off the screen to that tell-tale, two second tune that is probably going through your head as you read. There is no doubt that anyone handling a Nintendo controller without ever seeing or playing *Super Mario Bros.* before could make it through the game without that experience. Learning is no different. Students will make mistakes. It is a given. These are the same students, who like me, would spend countless hours of their real lives losing virtual lives over and over and over again. But eventually, all that messing up leads to a discovery, a moment of overcoming, a success, and we make it past what was holding us back from the next level. Again, learning is no different.

What makes a student willing to face digital death again and again, and be okay with it? Yes, I know it's a game, and games speak to another part of our brains, perhaps the parts that are addiction-prone, and all that stuff. But, why don't we view mistakes differently in our classes to create a culture that says mistakes are not only okay to make, they are moments to celebrate? What would happen if mistakes were just another part of learning, a way for us to discover something new instead of marking something wrong? Think about mistakes. They are sometimes the only way we *can* learn some concepts and skills. So, why the stigma? Celebrate mistakes, their realization and their reconciliation, just as much as any "right" answer given in class.

Help students see mistakes as part of the process. Mistakes, just as successes, lead us to other choices along the journey. We learn from them, no differently than we learn information from a text or a skill from a guided practice. What would happen if we cheered for mistakes in our learning? What if we celebrated those moments and took advantage of that excitement of a misstep in order to see new possibilities? Making mistakes matter as part of your students' classroom culture can be a real game changer. Pun intended.

Students Need to See They Learn Better with Others' Help

We are letting our students in on the secrets of what learning is, to whom it belongs, how to own it, how hard it is to work through, and what to do when those eventual mistakes happen. But, we have to instill one more vital practice into our collective learning values, and it's one some traditional classrooms find the most difficult in managing. Collaboration is king and key to getting learning to levels you've not experienced in your classroom.

Think about it, most of us as adults do not enjoy learning in solidarity. We dread sitting and getting in a professional development where we do not interact with our peers, share information, or work together on a prompt. We are social creatures, and we enjoy being social when it comes to learning. Learning deepens and expands when we are allowed to share experiences and perceptions in what we know and can do as teachers. If we all know it to be true in our own learning, why, oh why, do we deny this opportunity when seeking to provide learning for our students? Maybe we don't make it a common practice because it's not how we typically were taught. Maybe it's a classroom-management issue. Maybe it's a confidence thing. Whatever the reason, we need to get a culture of collaboration established, not only to improve learning in students, but to take some of the workload off teachers as well.

Sounds great, but how? You can start with the very same values you've been reading about that need to be instilled in students and established in classrooms. Maybe, if students knew what learning was all about, they would have a purpose behind collaboration during a lesson. Knowing what learning is, what it takes, and what they value in it, students can hold each other accountable in the process together. When they know that it's their learning, they might want to seek out other perspectives, options, and opinions from peers. Maneuvering in that hard work of learning, students may know they are not alone in the journey and seek out assistance, working together to face challenges, overcome obstacles, and even reflect on the progress. Even better, when they make those mistakes, they know they aren't making them alone and can find celebration and solidarity in turning those missteps into mastery. Establishing this type of classroom culture takes time, patience, constant shared accountability, but collaboration is also fostered on our end by designing for it to happen and happen effectively.

Ready to Jump in?

As I just said, we can have all these values and beliefs as teachers, and we can instill all these promises and practices in our students, but that's only the beginning of the process. All of the above are not necessary prerequisites to designing learning, but they will help you in the process. Initiating in this endeavor is different work. It will make you frustrated, it will stretch your thinking, it will challenge your conceptions. However, knowing that the real job of education is learning, what that requires of you, both mentally and emotionally, is well over half the battle. Having students on board as part of the process only makes the work lighter and more successful in the end. Please check out the resources located in Chapter 8, "Tips, Tools, and Templates," if you want to know more on how to begin. So, now that we've explored the prep work involved in stopping teaching, let's start designing learning.

Questions to Consider

1. What gets in the way of change the most as it relates to improving what we do for students in the classroom? The system? The staff? The students? Why?
2. What is a single aspect from what's needed from teachers that you already see in yourself as being a strength? Why?
3. What is an aspect of what's needed from teachers you feel will be most challenging? Why?
4. How will fostering what's needed to instill in your students be challenging? Is there one aspect that seems more difficult than another?
5. Would learning happen at high levels regardless of any of these qualities being present in our students and staff? Why or why not?

Reference List

Corwin. (2021, August). *Visible learning Meta*[x]. Retrieved September 7, 2022, from www.visiblelearningmetax.com/

DuFour, R., DuFour, R. B., Eaker, R. E., Many, T. W., & Mattos, M. (2016). *Learning by doing: A handbook for professional learning communities at work*. Solution Tree Press.

DuFour, R., DuFour, R. B., Eaker, R. E., Mattos, M. A., & Muhammad, A. (2021). *Revisiting professional learning communities at work: Proven insights for sustained, substantive school improvement*. Solution Tree Press.

Hattie, J., & Yates, G. C. R. (2009). *Visible learning and the science of how we learn*. Routledge.

3

Start Designing With the End

Design Incorporates a Functional Framework

Hopefully, after the previous chapters, you have come to the realization that the best way to ensure that learning is taking place in the classroom is through designing for it to happen. We can teach our hearts out like we have been, buy all the specialized learning programs and software available, come up with all the interventions possible to try and meet the needs of our students, but if we don't have well-designed learning as the base, we are in for a struggle. Here's what we need to discover: there is no way to spend, program, or intervene our way out of subpar Tier 1 instruction. But, we can design learning that does. All the money, programs, and interventions are pointless, ineffective, and inefficient if the learning we are providing as the basic standard is not at its highest quality. Quality that is driven by our intentional, instructional choices based on impact and effectiveness inform us as teaching professionals on what learning requires and make that part of the design we implement.

The framework we will be operating in for the rest of our journey has been around for a long time. So long, in fact, I cannot remember exactly its origin. However, it is one that allows for intentional design choices to be made that will impact learning in a way everyone (teachers and students) can see happening in the classroom. We will get into more specifics as we move forward as far as time and function are concerned, but for now let's just

DOI: 10.4324/9781003365914-4

generally define the parameters moving forward as *The Opening, The Instruction, The Work Session,* and *The Closing*. Again, while this common format for a framework may not be new to some of you readers, what may be new is the perspective you will soon gain behind the use and value of each component as we discuss their use in designing learning for students. More on this as we journey together.

More About a Common Format

But, there's an added benefit for students in using this common format as well. It lies in the fact that if we do want students to be a part of this process of learning, and we want for them to be aware of what learning is and what it requires, it helps that they are also familiar with a framework. Think about it. Right now, a typical middle or high school student may change classes four to seven times in a given school day – elementary and primary much fewer if at all. How much would be taken off the cognitive load of our students if they knew that learning in my room had basically the same structure and cadence as the science class down the hall and the math class upstairs? What could students get accomplished if they didn't have to relearn what learning was in every room they visited from day to day, year after year? Having a common format for learning helps ground things for students to enter into the environment, knowing what to expect and being ready to interact with their learning rather than relearn structures and rules.

The common format can also benefit teachers. We have a lot of teachers in need of support. Again, I was never exposed to anything that taught me how learning happens or how to build in qualities in my lessons to best promote it, and I graduated college with a teaching degree. There are thousands of teachers entering the profession without a teaching degree. In both these cases, teachers can use a blueprint off which to work, design, and be successful in constructing lessons that result in learning in the classroom. Teachers everywhere need support in designing learning. Part of that support lies in providing to them what success looks like in regards to quality lessons. This format helps provide this support, guiding teachers through the intentional choices necessary to improve what we do in the classroom.

Doesn't Stifle Creativity

Anytime I am part of a discussion on any type of "framework," the argument always arises about how something that tells teachers what to do, and when, will limit the creativity on the teacher's part to come up with the most engaging lessons possible. I get the concern. I was never one who liked to be "told" what to do in my classroom. I hated anything scripted, disliked reading the same old texts, and would bang my head against a wall before assigning the same writing prompts. However, this framework doesn't do anything to diminish a teacher's creative impact at all. I liken it to this: an artist has a canvas on which to create a masterpiece. He knows the size of the canvas to begin with and realizes he must operate within that parameter. Da Vinci could not stray off the canvas, hoping somehow to capture more of what the Mona Lisa was wearing. It's no different than the art some of our most famous athletes have displayed as well. Michael Jordan can do magically creative things with a basketball on the court, superhuman at times. His art in dunking, jump shots, layups, and the thousands of other choices he has are still limited to the rules and dimensions of the court. What you will see is that this framework will allow you to reach down even further into your creative bag of tricks because now, your creativity has an additional purpose behind it. You'll fine-tune your creative choices into even more engaging opportunities than you ever had before. You will be designers of learning.

Builds in Impact

So we have this framework in which to operate that is common for students and doesn't hold back any creativity, but what about the learning? Isn't that what this whole design concept is supposed to be about? Exactly. Design, like we said before, is about a means to an end, is about making specific choices with intended outcomes, and the ends and outcomes we want are all about learning. In Chapter 8, you will find the Tips, Tools, and Templates corresponding with each chapter. There you discover some tools that will assist you in the designing for learning process. There are also examples of how these tools can be used at different grade levels and content areas. As part of the supplementary materials for this chapter, you will find a copy of the Design Framework for you to reference as we continue our journey in making intentional instructional decisions about what happens in the classroom.

What I want you to notice about the framework is all the possible impact that has been labeled. Think about the previous chapter. We have to know the impact and use the impact to learning's advantage. We have so many students entering our classrooms in need of more than the typical one-year's growth from one-year's input. Some students are years behind in learning for a variety of reasons, which is all the more reason to make the purposeful, intentional design choices we need to make to get the most out of the opportunities we design for our students in the classroom. And remember, these practices of impact are not "one and done" types of actions. Remember that in order to be most effective on learning, they must be done often, well, and long-term. If we want these impacts to work, we have to use them on a consistent basis, to practice them with the highest quality, and to keep them as part of our learning all year long. We have to make these choices for our students and for ourselves. Having a design framework with several high-impact, universal practices built in only makes the job easier and more effective.

Order of the Design vs Order of the Delivery

Although the in-class delivery of the Design Framework chronologically flows from the Opening to the Instruction to the Work Session and finally to the Close, the order in which the design is composed is a little different, and for good reason. It's no different than how I taught writing to all of my students, elementary through college. We've all been there at some point. We've been presented with some type of prompt eliciting an extended written response from us, whether it was some standardized test, essay, college exam, or the like. How many of us have stared at a page or computer screen just waiting for something to come to us, anything to start this thing off? Like many other English teachers faced with the challenge of getting students to be successful at academic writing, I had my students step out of the chronological for a minute and into a design for writing based on reasoning. Students practiced answering the prompt in one sentence, then they were instructed to go right into the body paragraphs of the response. After writing the body of the essay, they then wrote the conclusion and introduction last. Why did this work?

Because it followed a reasoning order of what the students knew to do, rather than the chronological (introduction, body, and conclusion) order of the finished essay. Students knew the short answer to the prompt. From there, they knew what they needed to write to support their answer. Eventually, they wrapped up the response with a closing. The only thing left, and probably the most difficult to write, was the introduction because it required a mixture of creativity along with writing cohesion. In the end, the result was a well-crafted essay despite the fact that it was composed out of order.

The following chapters discuss the design of learning in a sequence most advantageous for teachers and not as it will be eventually delivered in class; the order of our design will flow as follows:

Design Order

1. The Learning Target
   a. What will the goal be for learning?
2. The Opening (Activators)
   a. How can I get them interested in this learning to start with?
3. The Work Session (Tasks and Assessments)
   a. How will I have students show their learning to themselves and to me?
4. The Instruction (G.I.S.T and Success Criteria)
   a. How do I prepare them for the task of their learning?
5. The Close (Summarizers)
   a. How can we summarize the progress of their learning?

Once designed with intent, purpose, and impact, we can rearrange these parts into the chronological order we are all familiar with in the classroom. Can you design in a different order? Without question. Some find that, like writing an effective essay introduction, that the Opening is the last decision in the design process. Some segments may feed into others more easily in your mind when making decisions. Whatever your design process eventually ends up becoming, the most important thing is this: each part has a specific purpose. The purpose is one that always supports learning. And our learning always begins with the goal or target in mind first.

Design Begins With a Target

Imagine this. Your supervisor brings everyone out to the front of your building, has the whole group line up side by side, and announces that the footrace is about to begin. Your supervisor raises a starter pistol and yells out, "On your marks! Get set! GO!" BANG! Look around you and what would you see? Some would stand there confused. Others may ask what's going on? I imagine even a select few may take off running in random directions.

The problem here is obvious. Even though your supervisor was perfectly clear on the fact this was a footrace and lined everyone up accordingly and went through the proper procedures to start the race, no one was ever told where the finish line was. Millions of our classroom lessons begin the same way.

In order for learning to be designed for effectively, teachers have to know and let the students know where the finish line (the goal) of learning is for the lesson. Our goal in the world of education is ultimately learning, so it makes complete sense to call these goals "Learning Targets." Learning Targets are essential for every lesson if you want to take your focus off of teaching and put it onto learning. Students need them. Teachers need them. The benefits of having them to build upon will make all the difference in what we provide in the classroom daily for learning.

Why Do Students Need Learning Targets?

Because without them, they would be standing at the starting line confused and unmotivated. Think about it from a student's viewpoint. If I don't understand what I am supposed to learn in the upcoming lesson, how am I supposed to focus any attention, energy, or mental resources on learning? What you are left with in regards to the classroom is a room full of students who set all their attention on what the teacher is saying and directing them to do, rather than on what they are supposed to be learning. That's the difference between teaching and learning.

Learning Targets also are an essential part of teacher clarity. Hattie's latest research puts teacher clarity at 0.84 effect size or roughly two years of potential growth (Corwin, August 2021). Clarity can be centered on three questions that both teachers and students should be able to answer: 1. What am I learning? 2. Why am I learning it? 3. How do I know I've learned it? (Fisher et al., 2021). In real-world-example classroom speak: *What?* We are learning about figurative language today. *Why?* We are learning about it because our learning today asks me to be able to cite examples of figurative language and explain their effect on text and its meaning. *How?* The Success Criteria will let me know. More on that later. But for now, imagine what students *could* learn, if they knew from the beginning where to set their sights on for their learning.

Why Do Teachers Need Learning Targets?

Learning Targets aren't only the bedrock for student learning; they also drive every single decision a teacher will make in regards to what happens in the classroom. They are the foundation of nearly all the curriculum and strategies that have the highest impact on learning. They drive what teachers choose to design tasks around, to pull resources for, to create assessments by, and everything else we want to accomplish for the learning of students. It makes sense for them to be called targets for our work as teachers just as much as it is for their learning as students.

Where do we begin then? It starts with your standards. Collective "Ugh" from the teaching masses. But, it's true. Your standards *are* your curriculum as a teacher, no matter where you are from. You are tasked and contracted to provide learning based on these standards. They are a list of what you "teach." Teachers, we have to dig into the standards in order to develop Learning Targets for your students and their learning.

Throwing a standard up and making that your target does nothing. Most are difficult for adults to understand, much less students. On that note, I've been surprised often that when teachers who actually commit to this process of standard analysis for Learning Target creation, they always discover they have been teaching a *lot* of unnecessary materials or missing out on some essential skills students need. Please, you will be tempted to scour the interwebs for those who have already completed this work in creating targets, but resist. Not to sound cliché, but this part of the design process really is about the journey, rather than the destination. Making a study of our standards for the purpose of Learning Targets will allow you to deepen your understanding, weed out unnecessary teaching, gain clarity on the mission in your classroom, and make sure you are really doing the job you have signed up to do.

Back to the purpose of Learning Targets, one standard often requires multiple, scaffolded lessons of learning before mastery can happen. This takes a lot of time and mental energy, I know. I am sure there are schools out there that have completed this work and hand out the list of targets correlated to standards for staff to utilize throughout the year. Whether your Targets have already been established and distributed or you have no Targets at all, I encourage you to do a complete excavation into the standards at least one time. The learning for us, as in most things anyone learns, lies in the process and the doing of the thing. The experience will result in learning.

Every time I have worked with teachers in decoding standards to identify Learning Targets, and I mean *every single time*, a teacher discovers something new. Whether that something new is something to add to their students' learning, something to take away, or even something they always believed was true about what they were teaching, but find out it really wasn't the case, teachers looking at the standards is always productive. With that said, I am going to attempt to bridge what I just wrote with the number one issue most teachers bring up in relation to what we are asked to teach as standards. There's not enough time. It is true. We don't have time to "cover" all the standards thoroughly. So, stop trying to do the impossible. So, how will defining Learning Targets help you as a teacher find more time?

Here's a practical explanation for why you want to create these targets. While it won't create more time, it will allow you to allocate more time to what is really important. Let's see how it works. You, and preferably other educators, collaborate together in decoding standards and creating Learning Targets. Now, you have a list of targeted learning for your students for this school year. Again, with a collaborative group, come to a collective agreement about these two questions: 1. What are the "*must have*" Learning Targets this grade level of students need before leaving you this year? And 2. What are the "*may help*" Learning Targets for the same students? What's the difference? Well, the *must have* targets are those students cannot leave you without mastering. They are the necessities of learning for this year. They cannot be overlooked, shrugged off, or brushed aside. They are the ticket to the next grade level. The *may help* targets, well they are ones that students can be exposed to, begin to develop, experiment with, dip a toe in before the year is out, but it will not be the end of the world if they did not quite master them.

So, you've decided on the must-haves and the may-helps. Put them in the order in which you would like to design your learning around for the students. What targets are prerequisites for others? What skills build on each other? Which are simple? Which are more complex? You are a professional educator, use your collective professional judgements and list the targets you have created in your determined order. You have now created a rudimentary "pacing guide" for your entire learning year. The rest falls right into place.

Next, decide where on this list you would like to stop and possibly gather large chunks of summative feedback on an assessment of some kind. Plan those out periodically. Design tasks for students to work through to show their mastery in learning. Gather resources, materials, tools, and anything else as you move throughout the chronological list of targets you have constructed. Or not – you can use this list just as easily in guiding students to do some of this work as well in their learning. The point is this: you have now established a specific set of skills you wish to center all your energies in design around, and you have a relatively solid order in which you want to accomplish this during the school year. Sounds like a great place to start.

So, to sum up. We need to develop Learning Targets as teachers. Not just for the students to have a clear finish to run towards during our classes, but for us to have a solid, intentional centerpiece on which to focus our mission. The learning target is the cornerstone for all design decisions you will make as an engineer of learning rather than a teacher of content.

Creating Effective Learning Targets

Derive from the Standard

We all have a curriculum. It's not one bought from a company, residing in a textbook or online platform. Our curriculum is *what* we are to teach. As far as I know, every state already has that established for us in the approved grade-level standards. That is what we are to teach. This is also where the design process begins. We must now take these standards and break them down into manageable learning. This learning, as Nicole Vagel states, must "tightly align to the standards, representing the learning students need to reflect the essence of the standard" (2015). Each standard has a lot of learning packed into them. It's our task in the design process to pull out the learning we are going to design for our students from these standards.

Include the Rigor

In the process of refining the standards into the Targets we want our learning to be designed around, we must make sure the rigor of the standard's original intention is met. We cannot lower the expectations of our learners. As we read earlier, we have to believe our students can learn at high levels and achieve the rigor of the standards. In other words, we cannot ask students to *identify* when the standard asks for them to be able to *analyze*. We cannot ask our students to *recall* when the standard asks them to *create*. We do not ever lower the bar. Our job is to raise our students to take on learning to reach the bar: to coach them up, to scaffold them up, to support them up. The standard is the standard. It's our job to get them there.

Exclude Any Specifics

Part of getting them there is being clear about the standard in the first place. Again, standards *are* our curriculum. Nothing else added. We want our Targets to be purely about the learning the standards ask for out of our students. My Target cannot be "I can determine the theme in the poem 'The Road Not Taken' by Robert Frost." Curriculum is what we teach; materials are how we want to teach them. When we confuse the two is when we get Learning Targets like this. Keep the materials out of the Targets. Stick to the standard itself. "I can determine the theme in a text." We want our students to be clear about what the learning is. We don't want any confusion about the clarity of the learning. Otherwise, students may think they only have to learn standards as they relate to certain materials or circumstances we provide. The journey has a destination, a finish line. Our students need to know reaching that goal sometimes looks different depending on our mode of transportation or different materials. But the goal remains the same regardless.

Write in Student-Friendly Language

If the student cannot understand where the finish line is, then they're going to have a hard time from the start. Writing Targets in student-friendly language is key. This involves taking that *adult* vocabulary sprinkled throughout the standards and bringing it to the level of the student. Again, we are not lowering or changing the standards, just making the language accessible for students. One great way to get this accomplished is through co-creating Targets with students, especially in our upper grade levels. Deconstruct a standard with your students, discussing the rigor and expectations of the standards, and together come to a consensus on what they need to be able to do in their learning. You will walk away amazed at what they can come up with. Regardless of your methods though, having the Target in accessible language is a must.

Break it Down to the Day

This quality can be a game changer for teachers as well as students. It can be a challenging one for the adults, but the benefits will be worth any extra mental efforts. When possible, break down your Target into what will be tackled by students during that day's learning. In other words, the journey to the Target's destination needs to be confined to today as much as possible. While the standard may say "Compare and contrast the point of view from which different stories are narrated, including the difference between first- and third-person narrations" (Common Core State Standards Initiative, 2022), today's Target, however, will be "I can compare the point of view of two different stories." Another lesson will be "I can contrast the point of view of two different stories." Eventually, we will do both together for another Target. The point is students need a clean, clear, and definable finish on a daily basis to celebrate and reflect upon in their learning. The next day can always bring references into previously attained Targets, showing connections and tying learning together even more for students. Chunking larger learning into more manageable pieces improves clarity and purpose, provides you with clearer pictures on where students actually are in their learning, and gives everyone the chance to celebrate progress and reflect on the process.

In Chapter 8, you will find a Learning Target Generator Tool as well as completed examples of their use. These forms are aimed at focusing our attention and questions on what matters most in creating Learning Targets from our state standards. I encourage you to use them, especially alongside other educator peers, to collaboratively generate Learning Targets for your students. Again, learning begins with a goal. The goal must not be a secret to our students. Let's make sure our first steps into learning are clear to all involved.

TABLE 3.1 Learning Target Success Criteria

Learning Target
I can create a Learning Target that:
• Is derived directly from the state standard.   • Includes the intended rigor of the standard.   • Excludes any specific elements not mentioned in the standards.   • Is written in student-friendly language.   • Is about the learning of the day.

Targets in Sight

Coming to the end of this chapter, you have arrived at the single most important initial aspect of design: the Learning Target. These Targets are the basis on which all other learning decisions will be made. They will be embedded into every other part of the lesson delivery. They are crucial in providing clarity, relevance, feedback, and so many other high-impact influences moving forward. Some of us have been teaching for years and feel we know exactly what our standards are asking in regards to the learning in our classroom. Still, it is imperative we reflect and reexamine exactly what our curriculum is and what our standards are asking in their highly dense and tightly packed statements. Others are new to teaching or new to the grade level or content being taught, and that is certainly a reason to dig into our state-curriculum standards and their purposes for learning. Once completing a complete unpacking, we can put Targets in order, establish an order, create a pacing, determine assessment plans, and so many other things necessary in designing a high-quality learning experience for our students for the school year in class. The next step involves discovering ways to tap into some of the energy students bring to classes during those opening minutes while beginning to tie our Learning Targets to everything we do as teachers.

Questions to Consider

1. What is your personal idea of a "plan" versus a "design?" Does this matter to what you do in the classroom?
2. What about the concept of design appeals to you from this chapter? What seems effortless and what seems challenging?
3. Have you ever "unpacked" or "deconstructed" your learning standards before? What has been successful in improving learning in your classroom? Why or why not?

4. What are some reasons why teachers wouldn't take the time to examine learning standards?
5. Do you think the need for students' knowing what the goal is before learning ever begins is important? Why or why not?

Reference List

Common Core State Standards Initiative. (2022). *English language arts standards "reading: Literature" grade 4*. English Language Arts Standards "Reading: Literature" Grade 4 | Common Core State Standards Initiative. Retrieved September 19, 2022, from www.corestandards.org/ELA-Literacy/RL/4/

Corwin. (2021, August). *Visible learning Meta[x]*. Retrieved September 7, 2022, from www.visiblelearningmetax.com/

Fisher, D., Frey, N., & Hattie, J. (2021). *The distance learning playbook: Grades K-12*. Corwin.

Vagel, N. D. (2015). *Design in five: Essential phases to create engaging assessment practice*. Solution Tree Press.

4

The Opening

The Opening

You have a Learning Target derived directly from the standard, posted in student-friendly vocabulary and class is ready to begin. The opening of a lesson is an exciting and extremely valuable time that every teacher needs to seize and maximize to its fullest potential. Here we will explore the true worth and work of the opening segment. My hope is that you will read this chapter and reflect on the design of the openings of your lessons walking away with new possibilities to try, new challenges to your current practices and new reflections to your craft when it comes to how to start learning off in the classroom.

What a Teaching Opening May Look Like Now

Let's be honest. If there is one area of teachers' lessons that has been neglected the most besides the closing, it would probably be the opening. It can often feel challenging when deciding on what to do in those few opening minutes of a lesson. There are a couple of archetypes of openings I have noticed in the classroom over the years, so let's look at some of the most common.

The "Mister Rogers" Opening
What I remember most about *Mister Rogers' Neighborhood* was the opening. We all know it. He enters that side door singing that

DOI: 10.4324/9781003365914-5

timeless tune, goes to the closet to grab the light sweater to change into, and completes this intro with his changing into sneakers and a friendly, "Hi, Neighbor." There are many classrooms that start this same way. The students enter the classroom and the opening task at hand posted on the board is some sort of ritual of readiness. Am I saying teachers need to throw out routines like this? Not at all! Many lessons cannot start without certain materials being armed at the ready like paper, pencils, interactive notebooks, and other supplies. The routine of students getting ready for learning to begin is necessary. However, if the ritual is the *only* thing the opening entails, then did we miss out on a great opportunity that matters to learning more than preparation?

The "Drill That Skill" Opening

I've seen many classes begin with a drill of some type. I know it sounds appealing and might even make sense, but perhaps there may be a better time or place for such a practice. I've been guilty of the practice myself. Things like Daily Oral Language skills, Word-of-the-Days, Math Skill Sets, Map Skill Practices, and the like are the bell ringers or warm-ups waiting on students every day from elementary to high school. Drills can be a good and useful tool to reinforce learning, but drills can kill learning as well if not applied at the optimal time and for the optimal reasons. Think about the purpose of practice. Think about when this might be most beneficial? Is it better to make this practice a disjointed introductory activity, or make practice like this (if you choose to implement) more intentional? Maybe there is a better time or place for them other than these precious opening minutes of the lesson?

The "Homework Hangover" Opening

Sorry to call you out, but you math folks are guilty of this more than any other content area. I have seen countless opening minutes burn out by students reviewing the previous nights' math problems together. I agree; it is an admirable practice to display the problems from the night before, ask the audience if they need assistance, and guide the masses through correct solutions. It is also a time for those who never did the practice for homework to get it done while it's being reviewed aloud. Some teachers use this time to wade through the rows of desks and check off that the homework was completed in the first place. Am I saying that you should not review homework? Again, no. But our job is to promote learning first. What does a student *learn* from this practice? It looks like they can learn to either do the homework at the surface level to be glanced over or to work quickly during its review to get the right answers. Do we want to spend this time in the opening scratching a surface of purpose or allowing students more worried about compliance than comprehension to just check a box in relation to homework? Can this be done at some other place or time to be more effective?

The "Opening That Never Was" Opening

This one probably needs no explanation. Some lessons begin with the students entering, supplies in hand, and the teacher begins the lesson. It happens a lot. Students come straight into a classroom and run right into a passive learning environment. At least with the other two there may be some sort of physical movement or human interaction. This opening is a motivational killer. Any hopes for getting students' brains primed and ready to tackle a Learning Target head-on after this opening has been squashed. Here's the crazy thing though, this looks good from the outside. I mean, what fellow teacher or supervising administrator wouldn't want to walk by this classroom and see an orderly room of students seated and a teacher teaching away? But was an opportunity missed along with the missing opening?

The opening you currently practice may be one of those common examples, some combination of them, or even something altogether different. Whatever your opening is, the litmus test that must be passed to measure its value is this: what is the goal of my opening today and what does it contribute to the actual learning in my classroom? My fear is we, teachers, use the opening as a transition to get ourselves ready while our students are busy. After all, we are about to have a lesson to teach. Or worse, we only have an opening because it is another compliance box to check off as complete. But what if I told you that openings are a powerful tool greatly affecting the learning to come during your instruction?

What the Opening Designed for Learning Looks Like

So, we admit our lesson needs some sort of opening segment to get things started. After reading about some of the typical teaching openings currently taking place in some classrooms, we can see a need. Great! Let's build from there. If you are a teacher who is dedicated to some of the warm-ups and bell ringers described previously, I will attempt to persuade you with some evidence. Let's look at some concrete evidence you don't have to consult a bibliography to see with the following question: teachers, when (meaning at what time of your lesson) are students the most energetic and excited? In other words, the most noisy and active. The bell ending class is not the answer. If you really look at your students, you will see they are most interested and tuned in at the beginning minutes of the class. The time before they must read, sit and get, or do anything that could potentially kill their interest and energy in the learning of the day. If this is true, we must ask: is the students gathering materials, sitting and working individually on a warm-up problem, worksheet, or reviewing homework really the way we want to take advantage of these valuable first minutes we have with them? Or, is there something else we can do to tap into all this potential energy and excitement? It appears we have stumbled upon our first design quality of an effective opening: engage with curiosity.

Engage With Curiosity

An obstacle we run into as teachers is that we have overcomplicated the issue of engagement with other purposes and clutter that don't have anything to do with engagement in the first place. Let's address the biggest misconception about engagement. Engagement is *not* synonymous with the word entertainment. Teachers, we think engagement requires some huge production, complete with song and dance routines, compelling dialogue, fireworks, and anything else by way of entertaining stimuli we can find.

While we may like our students to feel entertained, that is not the goal. The goal is engagement, and not just in the Opening. We want engagement throughout the entire lesson. Engagement is about developing an urge for students to want to get involved in whatever is going on in class. Getting involved in the learning is exactly what we need from our students, not to sit back and be passively entertained. One big difference that engagement has over entertainment is the motivation of curiosity.

We are curious creatures. We are attracted to things that are not of the ordinary. It is our nature to pay attention to things that grab our interest in this way, work to figure out a meaning or logic behind them, and try to fit it in with what we know to be true. It's an internal challenge, driving us to put our physical, mental, and emotional energies into focusing on the subject that has piqued our interest. There's no better way to open each and every class session with anything, no matter how big or small a production, that draws students' curious natures to the front and center. Corwin (2021, August) defines curiosity (with an effect size of 0.90) as this, "Curiosity relates to the urge to explain the unexpected, to resolve uncertainty, or the urge to know more." Isn't that exactly what we want out of students? The urge to know more? Use it.

What if we designed our Openings creating that urge in our students? Again, it doesn't have to be complicated in the slightest. For example, if a Target for a class of middle school math students is, "I can use variables to create an equation to solve a problem," I could have a box a vermicelli on my desk with questions on the board, "How many strands of spaghetti would it take to reach from one side of the room to the other? From here to the state capital? From here to the moon? Get with a partner and figure this out!" Students would be all over this. Why? Because no one would ever think to calculate the distance from one point to another in vermicelli units. It is a truly bizarre question. That is the appeal. But, just in case this type of information would ever be asked as the million-dollar question on a quiz game show, I have to find out for myself. Now, we can discuss how students arrived at the answers together: their methods, logic, reasoning, etc. All I have to do now is tie what they just did to what the Target is for the day, moving into the Instruction while also showing students they already may know more than they think they did about today's learning. Engage students, fostering the urge in any curious way possible.

Integrate With Prior Knowledge

There's another potentially impactful practice to put into place in the opening minutes of a lesson. It has to do with a subject most of us did learn in those college educational psychology courses we had, and it's probably the best design quality to put to use at the beginning of class. Let's consider things chronologically for just one second. A lesson at some point will include a teacher having to present new information of some kind. In other words, instruction happens. Now, we expect students to take our instruction, learn from it straightaway, and apply it to the work we have prepared for them to complete. But, if there was one thing I remember from those two education classes I had as an undergrad, it is that learning we want to stick does not happen that way.

All the way back in 1977, Anderson and Spiro introduced education to schema theory, which basically states we, learners, take in new information and assimilate it into the big interconnected web of knowledge and beliefs in our head already, the schema (Anderson et al., 2019). Every education major has heard this over and over, so why don't we try and do more with it, especially at the beginning of our lessons? In 2004, Marzano said one of the key ways students are successful in learning new content is building on the foundational knowledge they are bringing into class about the subject. Hattie and Yates (2009) also saw the connection to prior knowledge as a motivator for students. Students want to engage with things they are already comfortable with and know a little bit about. They will take the risk, getting involved in that learning as well as pay attention because there is a possibility to learn more. Corwin's Visible Learning research finds that a strategy to integrate with prior knowledge has an effect size of 0.93, which is over two years of potential growth (2021). So we see that this prior-knowledge thing does have some positive learning effects, right? With this in mind, let's think for a moment. Should we try and find a way to get students thinking about what they might already know about the information about to be presented, so that it is primed and ready to be used to attach something new to it? It makes sense, doesn't it?

Consider this analogy from the kitchen. There are two types of cooks: those who gather all the ingredients and materials together prior to getting started, and those who spend their entire time in the kitchen bouncing from the pantry, to the fridge, to the stove, and back to the pantry. I am the former; my wife is the latter, which is why we struggle cooking together. It is also why while I am cooking and nearly done, the kitchen looks like no one has been in there at all. On the other hand, my wife has flour on the floor, cut-up vegetable scraps on the counter, and almost every cooking pot we own out and going. Granted, the finely prepared meal gets to the table in both scenarios, and we remain happily married despite this culinary complication. In my mind, why not gather everything you need beforehand, so you are ready to cook? It's why there are currently over 15 meal-kit-delivery websites (yes, there are that many). These companies gather all the ingredients in measured-out portions, package them all together in a neat little box, and all you need to do is open the box and start cooking.

What if we designed moments at the beginning of class where our students gather their intellectual materials together, and dug them out of their mental pantry and fridge, so they can spend most of their time later simmering in their learning instead of running all over their mental kitchen trying to get things together? After that extended analogy, hopefully you can see there is a logical reason to activate prior knowledge at the beginning of a lesson.

Preview With Upcoming Content (If Necessary)

Sometimes, the learning of the day requires just a moment where we need to preview some information in order for students to access what they need. Every once in a while, students can be preloaded with vocabulary or skills so that when we get to the Instruction or the Work Session of the day, the focus will be on the true Target of the learning instead of something else.

Here's an example: let's say I ask you to check out your phiz. First of all, you have something on your ganthion. There, you got it. Also, you have a little bit of build-up in each of your canthus. Must have been a rough morning. Don't make your supercilia do that. I am just trying to help you out. There's a grin. Boy, when you smile your zygomas really show out.

These few sentences would be hard to understand for most of us. Although this might be an action we all do at some point during a given day or week, it sounds almost foreign because we are unfamiliar with the vocabulary. But, if I had given you some terms along with accompanying definitions, or better yet, visuals, of what each confusing word was, you would have a much easier time with the passage. If you knew your phiz is your face, your ganthion is your chin, your canthus is where your upper and lower eyelids meet, your supercilia are your eyebrows and your zygomas are your cheeks, you may have been able to access my instructions more readily. By the way, go look up what your philtrum is so you can impress others at a party.

Sometimes though, it's not about vocabulary. It might be a process or skill students need to be aware of before entering into learning. Other times, you might even want to ask students to bring up what they may already know about a subject as a pre-requisite before learning. For example, share out a Google Doc with the left column listed in rows of A-Z. Now, students take a quick five minutes to fill in the column to the right of each letter with whatever they already know about the phases of the moon, beginning their statements with the corresponding letter. This not only allows for a quick preloading of facts for students beforehand, it also allows the teacher to see what knowledge, terminology, or skills are mastered, or are lacking, before moving forward into the deeper learning of the concept. Again, while this function of an Opening is not as essential as the other previous two, it can be used in such a way as to promote engagement and access prior knowledge all at the same time.

Connect With the Target

There is only one thing left to do before we leave the Opening. We must make the connection between whatever we just chose for students to do and what the Learning Target is for the lesson. Otherwise, students may think they just engaged in something interesting or fun just for entertainment's sake. Remember, the Learning Target drives every single aspect of the lesson design. This is the first time you will reference it with students, so we have to make sure the goal is established and connected to all that we do together.

Some may ask, "Do I need an Opening every day?" My response would be, "Why not?" Personally, I have found it beneficial to break down learning into chunks that are able to fit within the confines of my assigned class time. Students tend to have better retention of concepts and skills this way. Anyone who was absent isn't walking into the middle of learning the next day. Designing these smaller learning opportunities always made more sense to me. But, for those who have learning that bleeds over into the next day, the answer is still, "Why not have an Opening?" It will allow students to reconnect with the learning from the previous day. It will tap into that energy they are entering the room with. It may allow you to check for the transfer of previous learning or address any prior misconceptions. Just as long as the Opening's purpose centers on what we discussed in this chapter, go for it!

Designed-Learning Opening Success Criteria

Moving forward, for each component of our lesson design, there will be success criteria included. This allows anyone who is in the room during this portion of the lesson to observe the qualities of an effective Opening. The great part about this is: this gives us what success looks like for the Opening through the lens of what we see the teacher doing *and* what we see the student doing.

As you can see, this table ties together all the elements we've been discussing in relation to what is effective in the Opening. The time is limited to 10% of the lesson. We don't want the Opening to take over the entire class time. There's more learning to be had, after all. "The Teacher will" column states all the things the teacher will do in the Opening. "The Student should" column are the behaviors and actions we expect to see in our students.

TABLE 4.1 The Opening Success Criteria

THE OPENING		
Time	*The TEACHER will:*	*The STUDENT should:*
10%	• Engage students' curiosity / involvement • Activate prior knowledge around the learning • Preview knowledge (if necessary) • Tie opening activity to the Learning Target	• Engage in opening activity • Access prior knowledge about the learning • Gain necessary prerequisite knowledge or skills • Recognize the goal of the Learning Target

While my personal "top picks" for the Opening in my classroom are described in the next section, please flip to Chapter 8 for many more examples that may be useful in your room. Do not let the list overload you. You cannot be expected to become a master of all these Opening activities. However, the advice I will give is to pick possibly five to seven to really put into practice. Some work better in a math class, while others work better in a science room. You will also find that some work better with first period while others work better in fifth. The goal is to make the Openings purposefully effective, and the best way to do that is for you to master a select few and put them into practice for learning.

Top Picks for the Opening

Turn and Talk

Chances are this one is not new to most teachers. However, it can be a no-frills, engaging approach to get students talking, connecting, sharing, questioning, and all the other idea-generating gooey goodness that comes with providing opportunities to collaborate. These talks can be for Targeted purposes depending on the questioning. For example, "Turn and talk to someone about all the ways you can figure out $1,108 + 246$ in your head," or "Turn and talk to a partner about reasons why plants are so important." One question is skill-based, while the other's purpose is knowledge-based. Formulate the question for your desired result.

If you are wanting some diversity in how students partner up, there are so many ways to do it: find someone with the same color shirt on as you do, partner up with someone who's birthday is even or odd just like yours, or Clock Partners. If you haven't experienced Clock Partners, it is an easy, yearlong way to establish partnering or groups, quickly and efficiently. Students can draw or are provided with a clock face. The numbers are labeled to the teacher's preference (I always stuck with the four majors: 12, 3, 6, and 9). Tell the students to find a twelve-o'clock partner and record the name under 12 on the clock. Repeat with different pairings for the remaining three times. Do this at the beginning of the year, have students keep them in a place for reference, and all you have to say is, "Get together with your three-o'clock partner."

There literally is no limit to what you can do with turn and talks. If you are wanting to pull up prior knowledge, they work. If you want to get students curious with an intriguing question or challenge, they work. They work because it allows students to talk and share ideas, which is one huge piece of what this learning thing is all about. The key is to make sure students know what a quality turn and talk looks like, feels like, and acts like. Once the expectation is easily set, turn students loose in sharing their thinking with each other, getting excited about what learning is on the way.

What-Ifs

I don't know if you have ever had this experience or not, but going toe-to-toe with a kid who likes to "what-if" every little thing that is brought up can be fun or it can be frustrating. A writing prompt I would use from time to time stated, "No student under the age of 16 needs a cell phone." Talk about opening the Pandora's box of situations and scenarios! I would get what-if-ed to death. From "what if I was kidnapped and put in the trunk of a car" to "what if I was attacked by a wild bear out in the woods," I would get every possibility imaginable. After listening to what felt like several hundred, I might eventually say, "What if a meteor fell out of the sky on top of us all right now?" and look up, staring for a few seconds. Eventually, students would start staring up as well, which would always crack me up. But, what-ifs can be turned around to ask questions and get our students thinking.

What I like about them is that we can design them in ways that engage the curiosity we want while also tying in any prior knowledge they might have about a subject. In a science class, I might ask "What if there were no bees?" And that's it. Kids might ask for more information, but all I keep asking with my hands in the air, shoulders shrugged is, "What if there were no bees?!" They can talk to each other or as a whole group, but we can get some common answers recorded to consider to tie to our learning for later. Sometimes, you can tie a what-if with another purpose to get students thinking. In language arts, I might ask, "What if there were no such thing as an adjective? Now describe your favorite flavor of pizza to someone nearby." I always loved making what-ifs about things like these because they are scenarios that most students had never considered before.

You can also use more reality-based what-ifs. Like, "What if you had $100 to spend on a pizza party for 30 people? Come up with three equations that, combined, use all your funds that cover 1) the pizza, 2) the plates and napkins, and 3) the drinks." How's that for relevance? Or "What if you had to design a model of how a wedge works? Pick no more than four items to include in your model." Again, what-ifs are about thinking and tying prior knowledge together while also getting students' attention with a completely absurd or unique inquiry, or one grounding them in reality. Either way, they are a great way to get learning jump-started in the Opening.

Sorts

If I had a favorite Opening activator, sorts would be it. I first learned of their potential after reading them in *Teaching in the Fast Lane*, by Suzy Pepper Rollins (2017). They can be used in a number of ways, they translate across all subjects and grade levels, and they can incorporate visuals, numbers, words, or anything you can imagine that could tie to their learning of the day. Sorts also can be designed to address all the thinking that great learning requires. They force students to evaluate, sequence, qualify, analyze, synthesize, compare, apply, question, and defend. Sorts can be individual, pairs, groups, or whole-class. They can be used most anywhere in your lesson, but I have found no more exciting place than in the Opening.

For example, I don't know about your school book rooms, but some schools I have served in were overflowing with old textbooks. My science teachers were about to begin entering the world of the classifications in the animal kingdom. My suggestion? Go to the book room. Cut up all the textbooks you want by finding pictures of a wide variety of animals. Take these images and throw them out on the tabletops for your students to sort into six different unnamed groups. Talk about engaging curiosity, tapping into prior knowledge, and using higher-order thinking. Groups had to come to a consensus and report out. What's even better is now this Opening activity can easily move into the Instruction by having students notice and list the qualities the examples in each group share. Who needs to take notes or definitions? Students will figure it out when we give them opportunities. I have completed similar sorts with examples of figurative language, equations, world governments. Again, the possibilities are endless.

But grouping or classification is not all sorts have to be about. Sorts can be used to identify sequencing, or cause and effect, like ordering the parts of the water cycle. We can use ranking sorts to justify relevance or importance, like ranking the causes of the Civil War. Two-sided sorts can be used as well, like determining which equations will have zero and which will have no solution. Again, there is no limit to how you can use sorts in your Opening. As with any activating Opening, pick your purpose and design it for that result.

Effective Opening Accomplished! What's Next?

There is no better use for these opening minutes in class than getting our students curious, predicting, guessing, asking questions, and developing the urge to be involved in the learning to come. Openings with strategies targeted at engaging the knowledge about today's learning that students are already bringing with them to class, while hooking that curiosity, are critical in setting the stage for what is next. Not only will the students seem eager to become involved, they will also have some prior knowledge on which to lean and feel more confident in the upcoming learning, as well as internal inequities already forming to guide them to seek out answers. Depending on our intention for the learning of the day, we may need to also incorporate the preloading of certain concepts, vocabulary, or skills in order to target what the learning really is about for the day without being bogged down by elements that are not essential, but require some type of understanding. Now that we have our Opening established, the next step in our design will leapfrog over what the typical natural order of a lesson is. While our lesson delivery will be moving into the Instruction portion, right now in the design process, we must first consider what our students will be producing for us to demonstrate their learning before we can consider what our role in providing instruction around that upcoming task will be. That is why what we must consider next is all about the Work Session.

Questions to Consider

1. Do your activities in the Opening fit one of the archetypes from the previous section? If so, do you see value in your current practice or do you feel it could be changed to better serve learning?
2. How important is the integration of students' prior knowledge to learning in your classroom lesson? Can you make do without it? Do you intentionally design for it to occur?
3. Do you feel engagement requires entertainment? Why or why not?
4. What do you find most challenging when considering what you want the Opening of your lesson to be? Why is this difficult?

5. What are your other thoughts about the Opening? Is it like your appendix? There, but not really being used for learning? Or is it a vital organ in the learning of your lessons? Do you want this to change?

Reference List

Anderson, R. C., Spiro, R. J., & Montague, W. E. (Eds.). (2019). *Schooling and the acquisition of knowledge.* Routledge.

Corwin. (2021, August). *Visible learning Meta[x].* Retrieved September 7, 2022, from www.visiblelearningmetax.com/

Hattie, J., & Yates, G. C. R. (2009). *Visible learning and the science of how we learn.* Routledge.

Rollins, S. P. (2017). *Teaching in the fast lane: How to create active learning experiences.* ASCD.

5

The Work Session

The Work Session

Many would naturally think the next step in the process after developing a Learning Target would be to answer the question, "Now that I know what I want students to learn, what am I going to teach?" But if we are going to be truly intentional with designing learning, we cannot jump right into what will be taught. Design requires more focus and purposeful choices than that.

The next, and I would argue the most critical, step in designing learning would have to be for teachers to answer the question, "What will students be asked to produce that "shows" me and them the Learning Target was met?" The answer to this question will be the center of every other design choice for a lesson. The Learning Task, or the product of student learning, is what students will produce by the end of the lesson that proves to the students and the teachers that whatever the "I can . . ." Learning Target goal states was actually accomplished. This is why the Work Session is so key to learning.

Learning is about the *doing*. Actually, the learning *is in* the doing. Most of the learning that occurs in the classroom is not when we have thought it happens all along. We think the learning takes place when the teacher is relaying information, giving directions, dictating notes, modeling processes, and all other things teacher-centered. But real learning takes place,

DOI: 10.4324/9781003365914-6

the kind of learning we really want from our students, right here in the Work Session. This is why this will most likely be the longest chapter – because most of the learning lies here. Learning happens when students confront the task designed for them and they struggle, make mistakes, reflect, and revise. Learning happens when they collaborate, work together to invent solutions, tackle something they have to question, use trial and error, share ideas, critically think, and communicate with others. This is the learning we want to see that helps develop all those other skills their future employers want to see as well. Our job as teachers (a.k.a. learning engineers) is to give them Tasks worthy of their learning, and that requires design.

What a Teaching Work Session May Look Like Now

The "You get a Worksheet, and You get a Worksheet, and YOU get a Worksheet" Work Session

The name says it all, *work*sheet. If these were about or inspired learning, they would be called *learning*-sheets. But, by nature, typically these worksheets are concerned with compliance and completion. Yes, they are most convenient for teachers and work well to manage a quiet and compliant classroom. But if you no longer wish to be a teacher and desire to become a learning engineer, then we have to rethink what we ask students to do as evidence of their learning. Some classes of students find themselves only ever completing worksheets as evidence of their learning. One after another after another and after another. Are ALL worksheets bad? Of course not. There are instances where a worksheet can help gather information, construct an organization, or produce research that all lead to a more rigorous and relevant Task. But if we are really honest about them, we can see they most often serve classes as pacifiers in place of true learning evidence. If we use worksheets, they must have a designed-for, rigorous, and relevant purpose for the work that will show learning, instead of being only about the work.

The "Read and Answer the Questions at the End of the Passage" Work Session

Surely, reading passages and answering comprehension questions are high-quality Tasks. I mean, this has been a staple of every text-book curriculum or workbook that I came up attending school completing. The impact on learning must be one that makes these types of activities valuable and successful, reaching high levels of achievement. In reality, they are nothing more than a work-sheet printed at the end of a text, chapter, or lesson. Many are about simply moving information from Pile A to Pile B. We have to expect more out of the learning opportunities we provide than that. It's passive, unengaging, and a learning killer. Do questions serve a purpose? Yes! Questions are paramount in the learning process. But the questions don't need to be ones simply answered to get an answer. Questions need to lead the learner to some-thing of value to their learning. Once there, the learner can take this new information and use it for a greater purpose. Guiding questions are great, but they need to guide learners somewhere where real learning can take place, instead of a destination where compliance in answering is the final stop.

The "Fun Without the Function" Work Session

There is nothing like the energy you get from visiting a classroom where all of the students are excited and immersed in whatever the teacher has provided as classwork for the lesson. The room is buzzing with students talking and working through some sort of activity. Kids are smiling, concentrating, working together. We adults are standing back, basking in the joy that is all students being engaged in the activity. Success! Well, maybe. Sometimes we provide what students consider to be a "fun" activity for their learning. The problem is that while these activities get students involved, they do not always provide the desired learning. It might be that we didn't connect the activity to the target for students. It might be that the activity doesn't provide true, student-centered evidence that learning took place. It might even be that the activity has nothing to do with a standard or learning in the first place. The function is missing from the Task. The function IS the goal because the function matters to how the task will show students their learning. Fun can be incorporated in what we ask of students in their learning, but we cannot ignore that the function is what gets learning accomplished. Our job in the Task at times is to put the "fun" in the "function."

The "EdTech Killed the Classwork Star" Work Session

With the golden age of technology we are entering, combined with the pandemic we've been experiencing, more students have access to and are using technology than ever before. The sad part is that many of the devices, iPads, and Chromebooks in their hands are in danger of becoming digital worksheets. Don't get me wrong, there is a lot of cool, interactive, and engaging stuff that Edtech can do and that students use every day in their learning. They are tools to bring experiences and innovations to the classrooms like never before. However, there are many who are still stuck in the "tried and true" methods of teaching and assigning the same old stuff when they could take the opportunity to design digital learning anew. I have walked by so many silent classrooms, even more so in the last two years, where students' heads are down, eyes glowing from the reflected light of their devices, and all of the materials, questions, guidance, interaction, and assessment is taking place on screen. It makes for a nice, quiet, compliant classroom, but we need to design ways to use Edtech tools in creating a larger, more learning-showcased Task, where students can work through, collaborate together, make mistakes, receive feedback, reflect on methods, and assess their products in relation to the target of the learning.

What a Work Session Designed for Learning Looks Like

The learning that lies ahead centers on what we'll call the Learning Task. In the designing learning process, this is the very next decision a teacher typically makes after choosing a Learning Target to construct a lesson around. I have a target, now what do I want the students to do that "shows" them and me that they have met the goal set for their learning? In other words, what can students accomplish that results in a product anyone can observe and identify that mastery of the Learning Target was achieved. Sounds pretty simple, right? It's not always that easy. There's a lot more that matters to what we give as work to students, and it requires design on our part.

Tasks Must Be Designed, not Just Assigned

That is the biggest difference between "work" and "learning products" students complete in class. One is concerned with compliance and completion; the other is focused on evidence and effectiveness. A quality Task has some basic, minimal requirements to meet in order for them to be effective in showing that learning happened. Too often we fall back on traditional practices that may hinder the students' and our own ability to see the learning taking place throughout the completion of the Task – reading a text and answering questions, for example. What about this practice is an outward, clearly ascertainable display of learning other than getting an answer correct or incorrect? Worksheets often offer the same difficulty and challenge when it comes to seeing the learning. Digital assignments, while appearing from the outside to be innovative and engaging, may really just be electronic versions of the same old same old.

This is why we must design Tasks and not just assign work. A well-designed Task takes a lot of preparation, collaboration, and investigation on our part. A well-designed Task should require a lot of the same on the part of the students as well. Weston Kieschink puts it best when he states that, "It is up to us to design activities that require students to take action and think about the action they are taking as they progress" (2022). We have to design work that promotes and produces learning. We have to identify quality work, to engage students, to anticipate misconceptions, to build equity, to provide feedback, and to make these Tasks do for learning what they truly should be intended to do. The Task carries with it and in it the lion's share of the learning.

Tasks Must Show Evidence of the Learning Target

The primary purpose of the Task is to provide something for the students to face, producing something that can be pointed to that demonstrates the desired learning actually happened. Like the "Fun Without the Function" example, our Tasks must have been designed with the Learning Target in mind. Not only that, we have to make the connection between what the students are being asked to do and the Learning Target. Otherwise, students miss the clarity component. No matter how fun or hands-on or collaborative an activity might be, if students cannot answer, "Why are we learning X?" based on what they engaged in during the Task, the mission of the classroom now has moved away from learning.

When you don't have that clarity piece, you also venture into less meaningful compliance instead of the actual learning you want to accomplish. You'll get the answer I got from some eighth-grade students in an English language arts class-room I walked in that was annotating text to cite evidence of the author's purpose. I asked them what they were learning today. The answer? We are learning about killer whales. Killer whales don't appear in any ELA standards that I am aware of. The kids were reading and underlining some things and making comments. Compliance in the work was there, but the learning was lost in the mix. Some may say that the response is an easy and acceptable confusion on the students' part. But, making the connections between everything we do in class, especially the Task, to what we are wanting students to learn is vital. If we missed making it here, chances are, we are missing it in other areas of the lesson as well.

Not only is the connection to the Learning Target essential to the Task, so is what comes as a result of students completing the Task. Remember hearing that deep philosophical question: "If a tree falls in the forest, and no one is around to hear it, did it make a sound?" Take a similar question to the classroom level and ask: "If a student receives a 100 on a worksheet, did learning happen?" At the end of the Task, there must be something sitting in front of us, both students and teachers, that everyone can point to and see that learning happened. There needs to be tan-gible qualities residing in this product that students can put their eyes and hands on to be able to explain exactly how they have proven learning today.

Students need to be able to look at that evidence, analyze it, and reflect on it. They need to be able to see what worked well, what was a struggle, what they need more of moving forward, or what changes they will make next time when facing similar Tasks. That is what learning is all about. It's never been about content and compliance. It has always needed to be about allowing students the opportunity to work through something, gaining insights along the way that they question, try, reflect on, challenge, evaluate, and revise. Not about the content they are learning, but about the learning process itself and the concepts involved in that. We must instill this type of mindset in our students about what learning is and what their part to play in it is, but we also have to design Tasks that allow them to see the Learning Target as well as reference the results.

Tasks Must Promote Engagement

Remember from the previous chapter, engagement is not about entertainment. Engagement is about an urge to become invested and involved. I would wager this is the most challenging aspect of our profession, and there is no place in our lesson where engagement is more of a challenge than in the Work Session. Why? Because this is where we really turn learning over to the students. We are not in the Opening with curiosity and energy still abounding. We are not in the Instruction, where the teacher is driving the learning and getting students ready. We are in the segment of the lesson where the Task must be one designed, targeting the specific needs promoting students' engagement at the student-driven level. This is a place where we can lose our students to passive or active disengagement, or we can have Tasks designed in a way to keep the urge alive in their learning.

So what does designing an engaging Task require? First, we have to make sure what we are asking students to tackle during the work session follows what Hattie describes as the Goldilocks principle of challenge. That means the Task needs to be "not too easy, not too difficult," but just the right amount of challenge (Hattie, 2012). When the Task is too easy, students may not see the relevance in it or may see the work as just something to keep them busy during class with no real learning value. That eventually transforms into boredom, and boredom has a negative impact on learning in the classroom (-0.33 effect size) and usually results in more behavioral issues as well (Corwin, 2021). After all, if a student isn't using energy in completing a challenging, a meaningful Task, then the energy has to go somewhere, and that somewhere is usually towards actions most deem as misbehaviors.

On the other hand, when the Task is perceived as too difficult, the chances of misbehavior increase for the same reason. The Task is too hard. Students shut down. Energy is transferred to less desirable actions in the classroom. How do we keep students from shutting down when the Task seems too difficult? We first make sure it literally isn't too difficult, obviously. But we also need other things in place during our Work Session to lessen the urge to shut down and strengthen the desire to be engaged. Some of that comes from other groundwork you have previously laid in your relationships with students. Students know that I'm here for feedback and help in their struggles, not judgment and correction. We foster, welcome, and love mistakes so that we can get better together. Some of the shutdown urge is thwarted by providing clarity, tools, and other safety nets students can access during the Task to work through and save themselves when things get tough. Their learning needs to challenge them, but challenges are not about defeat. Challenges are seen as winnable from the start, and we must make sure we aren't consistently handing students defeat along with their assignments.

The other key to designing engagement into what we ask students to do for the Task is making sure we design qualities that attract students. Remember, it's about the urge. Not many worksheets create an urge other than the one that is about balling it up and tossing it into the trashcan. What creates the urge in the Task or work we provide? After all, do students really *want* to do the work? They do and they will when we purposefully make Tasks appealing. Antonelli and Garver's research in this area found there are eight qualities that could be incorporated in Tasks that appeal to students and promote engagement. These qualities are: Clarity, Personal Response, Sense of Audience, Safety, Collaboration, Choice, Novelty, and Authenticity (2015).

Out of the over 17,000 classroom observations they conducted, Antonelli and Garver discovered these qualities were most effective in getting and keeping students engaged in the Task.

Right now you are asking yourself, "How in the world am I supposed to incorporate all of these qualities into everything I design to assign my students?" That is the other beautiful part of their research findings. They discovered that if an assignment contains the minimum of three of these qualities, the results are that 87% of the students will be engaged in the Task (Antonetti & Garver, 2015). How amazing is that?! Engagement is a necessary condition we account and design our Tasks around because the learning happens here, and our students need to be involved, since it is their learning after all.

Tasks Must Bring Equity to the Learning

I'll remind you here of the analogy from Chapter 2. Our students come to us in a vertical line outside our door. Those in the front of the line come to us with different exposures from home life, materials, previous classrooms, and other factors that make accessing learning a shorter journey for them. Those in the back of the line have a longer distance to cover to reach the learning. What's our job then? To do whatever it takes to rotate that line, turning it to a place where learning is equally accessible to all, regardless of what they enter the room with or without. That's the beginning of equity.

What students entering have or do not have is really out of our control. But, there is something that we have complete control over that must be addressed in order to move toward achieving equity for all: our response. Back in Chapter 2, the phrases, "These kids can't" and "These kids won't" were really direct quotes I have heard over the years from my peers. There is some truth to those statements, and here it is: the second the teacher utters them, internally or aloud, they become true through the choices and actions of the educator. What I mean is this, if we don't believe certain students can learn or want to learn, then we immediately find ways to lower the work/assessment/task/bar to meet them where we think they are. This is the opposite of equity.

Our job is to do whatever it takes to raise these kids up to be able to meet the level of the standard in the Task we design for them to do. The standard *is* the standard. We can't change that. Our job is designing learning, resulting in students reaching that standard. If the standard in fifth-grade social studies is to "Analyze the main features of the New Deal," then everyone in the room is expected to be able to do that. How students accomplish this learning goal may need to look different for equity to be achieved.

For example, the Task requires all student work resulting in a product that shows this standard was met; however, *how* this will be accomplished may look different. These students have one reading selection on a preselected Lexile level. They have guided fill-in-the-blank statements to complete based on the reading and will have a guided end product that demonstrates their learning. Another group may have three to five resources to reference during the Task, guiding questions provided leading them to essential information, and a choice of two methods of presenting their findings and understanding of the New Deal. Still another group of students may have ten resources from which to choose, students determine what the important information to use will be, and a Choice Board including eight products to pick from to demonstrate their analysis of the New Deal.

This is what scaffolding and differentiation is about. They are about providing equity, so that all students in the room have equal access to the learning of the day. Everyone in the room is meeting the same learning, but the tools and pathways used by each student to get there are different. Kids shouldn't have to reach farther than others in the room to touch learning. It's our job to design Tasks so every child's reach, regardless of how they arrive to us, results in the same learning as everyone else in the room. That's our job. We come together, collaborate, bringing all our shared expertise and experience, and figure out what tools, resources, and pathways we can design into our Tasks to get this accomplished. We keep bringing them to our students until we find the ones that work best. We expect all our students to learn at high levels as a result. We don't settle for anything less, out of them or out of ourselves.

Tasks Must Provide Escapes and Pathways

If I had to pick one element of a well-designed Task that benefits the teacher in the classroom the most, it would be this one. While tools and pathways can be used to provide needed scaffolding, and differentiation when needed to provide equity for our students, they can also serve in taking more of the workload off of the adults in the classroom as well. If we really want to turn learning back over to whom it belongs, designing Tasks with included Tools to Escape and Pathways to Accelerate are ways to make this a reality in our rooms. While we will discuss their use more in the next chapter about the Instruction, they must be included in our discussion about the essential elements of a quality Task in the Work Session.

Tools to Escape: what happens when a student gets stuck in their learning, has a question, or needs assistance? Typically a hand goes up. Where there is one hand, there will be another, then another. As the teacher, you are running around the room trying to get to all the needs you can. But, what if there was a better way? What if we had things specifically designed and ready for students to access while working on the Task that helps them get unstuck? What would happen is students, knowing the Target and what success looks like, will take the tools you've designed and provided for them, and work with and through them in order to overcome the obstacle in the way of their learning journey. This is what ownership is in learning, and it's vital that we give our kids the opportunity to take it on.

Pathways to Accelerate: what about those students who've "got it down"? Those who are ready for more and want to take the learning deeper or to the next level? If we don't have something ready for them to take on in the Task, they could become bored, seeking to use energies elsewhere. Their hands will go up around the room as well, only instead of a question, they will be responding with an "I'm done." They have no place to go in their learning if we don't provide a pathway for them to take. Pathways are not about more work, they are about deeper challenges. Tasks must have pathways beyond meeting the standard students can take to explore, explain, extend, and expand their understanding of the learning. Otherwise, we are doing them a disservice and taking on more work for ourselves.

Tasks Must Allow for Quality Feedback

As teachers, we are constantly giving feedback whether we realize it or not. Some of our feedback is the positive praise we give when a student answers a question aloud during class. Some of our feedback takes the form of follow-up questions to students during a discussion. Still more common is the feedback students receive after completing an assignment: feedback that typically is colored red along with a numerical value at the top of a paper. However, feedback can be a powerful tool in learning if we choose to design for its use and tap into the potential it has for students' learning.

Again, we are thinking about feedback as it relates to what we are providing students to demonstrate their learning for all to see. To tell you the truth, I was guilty of providing the same, surface-level feedback that many of us are guilty of when it came to my students. Nearly all of my feedback came in the form of praise like "Good job!" and "Great work." Still more was, "Go look at that again," or "Is there another way to think about this?" And of course, the grade on the paper at the end of it all. Going back to my apology in the introduction of the book, I really didn't know any better, because that's what teaching and feedback looked like to me from being a student in the classroom to becoming a certified teacher. Are there times for the positive, surface-level praise responses to students' results? Yes. Are there other times we need to ask follow-up questions to help guide them? Absolutely. But, if we want feedback to stick with our students and really make an impact, we have to design for it to happen during the Work Session and the Task.

Feedback, the impactful kind we want to provide as part of the students' experience in the Task, requires three main elements be in place: a Learning Target, Success Criteria, and Student Evidence. Think about it this way. Our job as the teacher is for students to reach their learning goals. So, students know the goal for their learning with the Learning Target. The Task has been assigned for students, and with it, Success Criteria that give tangible, observable traits on what quality learning looks like for this Task. Finally, as a result of the Task, students bring forth evidence that they produced to demonstrate their learning. So now, what do we do as teachers to provide quality feedback?

Looking at the evidence with students, we guide them in comparing it to the Success Criteria. We ask questions like, "Where do you feel you are at in your learning right now based on what we're looking at?" or "Let's talk about your next steps in your learning while we look at the Success Criteria together." We must tie their evidence to the success criteria and eventually back to the target for feedback to work. In other words, your work shows you are here, your goal is to go there, and now here's what we can do to get you there. Designed in various ways, feedback can even be a collaborative effort among students, not just relying on the teacher to be the sole provider. So what does quality feedback give us? According to Corwin, feedback's effect size is 0.62 when it is given to students "regarding aspects of one's performance or understanding that reduces the discrepancy between what is understood and what is aimed to be understood" (August 2021). In other words, students through their Tasks are showing what they know now. Teachers provide guidance, tools, support, feedback that closes the gap between what they are showing and where the goal for learning is, paving a clear path on how to get there.

Designed Learning Work Session Success Criteria

TABLE 5.1 The Work Session Success Criteria

THE WORK SESSION		
Time	The TEACHER will:	The STUDENT should:
50%	• Facilitate the independent or group work on the Task. • Purposefully assign collaborative groups and differentiated Tasks based on formative assessment from mini-lesson. • Monitor, assess, and document student performance.	• Engage independently or collaboratively with the Task. • Demonstrate proficiency in skills and concepts related to the Learning Target. • Self-assess using success criteria and explain progress using standards-based vocabulary.

TABLE 5.1 (Cont.)

THE WORK SESSION		
Time	*The TEACHER will:*	*The STUDENT should:*
	• Redirect students to tools to escape and pathways to accelerate. • Allow students to struggle, make mistakes, and conduct error analysis. • Conference with students. • Provide standard-based feedback referring to established success criteria and Learning Target.	• Utilize tools to escape and pathways to accelerate. • Struggle, make mistakes, determine course of action in learning, and analyze errors. • Conference with the teacher to receive feedback tied to the Learning Target and success criteria. • React to feedback, make adjustments, reflect on learning, and progress to target.

My Top Picks for the Work Session

RAFTs

If there was a Task that translates to any content area or any grade level, a RAFT is it. They can demonstrate understanding of any area of learning on multiple levels while also allowing for creativity, personal response, and choice that promote engagement in students. Their use can only be limited to our imagination.

A RAFT is essentially a writing assignment, but can be modified into any form of product. The acronym stands for:

R- Role of the writer (who are students pretending to be?)
A- Audience for writing (who are students writing to?)
F- Format of the writing (what type of writing is it?)
T- Topic of the writing (what's the writing about?)

Some examples:

- High school United States history. Students in class might be asked to play the role of Colonial America writing the British Crown a letter on how they need to end the relationship. In other words, a break-up letter from America written to England in 1776. Students can demonstrate their understanding using sources like the Declaration of Independence and other historical events of the Colonial period in order to write the letter while playing the role. Part of demonstrating success on this Task is the use of evidence supporting America's reasons for the split. Students are encouraged to be as creative as possible in their writing.

- <u>Middle school life science</u>. Students can play the role of a butterfly, writing a lullaby for a younger caterpillar who is afraid of forming a cocoon and going to "sleep." The lullaby will be about all the changes and the future lying ahead for the caterpillar, including all relevant conceptual understanding and vocabulary.
- <u>Middle school math</u>. Students can be the Decimal Point who is currently running for Mathematical President. The prospective voters want to hear the reasons why Decimal is so influential and important to all the other numbers and math functions, and why it deserves their vote during a campaign speech. Conceptual knowledge required, along with real-world examples, could be used to demonstrate learning.
- <u>Elementary reading class</u>. Students in a first-grade reading class can respond after reading the book *David Gets in Trouble* by David Shannon. Students are drawing pictures with a helpful sentence below the picture. These how-tos are written for the kindergarteners who might need help in making good choices at school by focusing on some common school scenarios kids find themselves in.

You can even take a RAFT to the next level by allowing students to choose each aspect of the assignment for their response as long as predetermined Success Criteria are available for feedback to occur. Again, RAFTs can be used for Tasks that can easily show understanding and learning of conceptual, procedural, and application knowledge. The success of our RAFT lies in our ability in providing the creative space in which students can operate while producing their writing, picture, poem, story, letter, or any other response. It also requires us to predetermine the type of evidence of learning we want out of our students. Do we want responses to show their understanding of a process, understanding of a concept, understanding of application of learning? Whatever the ends we desire, a well-designed craft can give us a creative means to allow students to demonstrate their learning in any classroom.

Choice Boards

Another popular and versatile Task for The Work Session is the use of choice boards. These can come in all shapes, sizes, formats, and functions. The first decision you need to make, just like anything else we choose for the classroom with learning in mind, is what do I want the purpose of this choice board to be? Is it a choice board for review and practice of fundamental skills? Is it one that has students evaluating different strategies or methods of completing an assignment? Or is it one I want to specifically aim at differentiating or scaffolding a Task for students? Like everything we choose to do, the end goal or purpose shapes the other choices we make.

These choice boards can be as simple as a 3x3 grid on paper or displayed on your board in the room. The activities of each board must have a purpose you have intentionally chosen behind them. Perhaps this 3x3 board is in a math classroom. The first column has three different choices all relating to solving a two-digit subtraction problem using a visual method like a number line or a drawing. The middle column has choices requiring the use of expanded form in some way. The last column has choices asking students to use a standard model or algorithm. Students are free to choose one item from each column as they work today on two-digit subtraction.

You can design choice boards that build on previous skills. I have seen these come in the form of mimicking a restaurant menu. Listed in the "menu" are the standard categories of appetizers, soup and salad, main entrees, sides, and desserts. The entire unit work may be designed around this menu concept. Staring with the appetizers, students are introduced to Tasks that result in their learning the preliminary information and skills that will be needed later on in the main entree. Soup and salad may add a few more prerequisites. The main entree could be a larger, more complex Task while the sides are choices of differing supporting skills and knowledge that could be used to assist them. Once completing the meal, students' desserts can come in the form of self-assessment, feedback on the process, or something else that aids in summarizing the learning. Each menu category has multiple choices, point values, or any other quality you wish to add as long as it is about the learning. Getting creative with this type of choice board, or any other type for that matter, is possible in any subject area or grade level. We just have to be intentional about it.

Real-World Scenarios

There is nothing like taking what happens in the classroom and connecting it to something real. I mean, didn't we all ask the same question back when we were in school that our students are asking us now, "When am I going to use this in real life?" Making what we do in the classroom applicable, relevant, and connected to life outside of the walls of the school only makes for a more engaging and authentic experience in our student's learning. Even if the real-world scenario we set up seems a little over the top like the one I am referencing in the next paragraph.

Attending a math conference a few years back, the educators in the room were asked, "What are the ingredients of a standard American cheeseburger?" We listed and discussed. Then, we were introduced to In-N-Out Burgers' menu options of 3x3 cheeseburgers, 10x10 and even higher. So the question was posed, "What would a 100x100 In-N-Out burger cost?" This question comes to us courtesy of Robert Kaplinsky (2021), and it really got us thinking in the room. There *is* an answer, but at first, all we were given was the question. Later on, we were shown a picture of the standard menu and costs. Eventually, we were shown a receipt displaying the charge for a 100x100 burger. This is something that exists out there in the real world, and we were determined to figure this out. Students are no different when we give them similar opportunities. I cannot tell you how many math standards you can address with this one problem. Extending it, adding more information, asking different questions among other tweaks can target any specific learning you target desires.

Another example could be when my ELA classes would be invited into the room, given Press badges and find that all of the seating which was normally in groups had been moved into rows facing the board up front. They discover that they are now movie critics for a local publication and have been invited to a movie premiere. Their task is to view some selected movie scenes and write up a review critiquing the director's choice of set design, lighting, cinematic shots, and sound. They must support their opinions with evidence, just as if they were writing about a text they may have read in class. After showing a scene, the students/movie critics were allowed to confer with one another, sharing observations and notes. Repeating this for a few scenes from the same film, they were eventually led to the writing of the review, complete with Success Criteria.

Why do these work so well for Tasks? Because they are innately addressing many of the design qualities for engagement we looked at earlier in the chapter. We have novelty, authenticity, clarity, personal response, collaboration, and more. But, I find they really work because it's something that students know about and know about from experience. They know what a cheeseburger is, how they are made, what one tastes like, and where to get one. They know what it's like to watch a movie sitting in a darkened theater or at home on the couch. These are things they have life experience with, not something they had to read in a book about. Coming up with these is just about taking what you want them to be able to know and do, connecting it to something that is commonplace in their lives, and making it interactive in some way.

You've Designed a Quality Task. Now How Will You Get Students Ready?

Tasks in the Work Session are where the learning happens. That's why we devote half of our class time to this segment of the design. This is where the students will be thinking, adapting, struggling, reflecting, revising, and all the other real and true learning practices that we want out of them. We, teachers, are busy in this moment of monitoring, conferencing, providing quality feedback, redirecting to tools and pathways, and facilitating the learning we have designed for students to take on and take ownership of. It's theirs after all, remember. The next step in the design process is to ask ourselves, "How am I going to get the students ready to take on this Task?" We will have to make intentional decisions about the information, skills, and tools we need to put in place for students as we move into designing the Instruction.

Questions to Consider

1. The majority of the learning takes place in the Work Session. Do you agree or disagree? Why?
2. What about designing an engaging Task seems the most challenging? What about it is difficult?
3. Considering grading of the Task, what is more important: the resulting number or the resulting learning? In other words, if a student earns a 100 on a Task, does that mean learning occurred? Support your answer.
4. Equity is central and key in designing a quality task for students. Do all of your students typically receive the identical assignment, responding in an expected identical way? If so, how can this be modified to provide equity for all your learners in reaching the goal?
5. What feedback do students in your room typically receive? Is it about right or wrong? "Fix this" or "that's good"? Or do you provide feedback that promotes reflection and revision to assist students in moving upward and deeper in learning?

Reference List

Antonetti, J. V., & Garver, J. R. (2015). *17,000 classroom visits can't be wrong: Strategies that engage students, promote active learning, and boost achievement*. ASCD.

Corwin. (2021, August). *Visible learning Meta^x*. Retrieved September 7, 2022, from www.visiblelearningmetax.com/

Hattie, J. (2012). *Visible learning for teachers: Maximizing impact on learning.* Routledge.

Kaplinsky, R. (2021, March 30). How much does a 100x100 in-N-out cheeseburger cost? *Robert Kaplinsky.* Retrieved October 6, 2022, from https://robertkaplinsky.com/work/in-n-out-100-x-100/

Kieschinick, W. (2022). *The educator's atlas: Your roadmap to engagement.* ConnectEDD.

6

The Instruction

The Instruction

In the design sequence, we've reached the point where we have a quality Learning Task for students to complete that is not too difficult, not too easy, but just challenging enough to be engaging. We have provided tools to utilize to escape misunderstandings, pathways to take to go deeper into learning, and methods to provide feedback. We've built a Task we can be proud of, so now's the time to move into what the essence of being a teacher is about, instruction. Isn't that, like, THE job of the teacher? It is really the one thing we get up there in front of the class and excel in. We instruct, teach, provide pedagogy, whatever you'd like to call it. But what if I told you, this really isn't the place where most of the learning is rooted in or where students "learn" the most? Is instruction important? It's vital to what is to come. What I want you to reflect on in this chapter is the true purpose and potential that resides in this part of your lesson design.

What a Teaching Instruction May Look Like Now

In the Opening, our students were engaged with curiosity, prior knowledge was activated, and now the class is transitioning into the moment the teacher provides what's needed for learning. Here is where we shine as teachers. We are ready, studied up,

DOI: 10.4324/9781003365914-7

pumped to give out the content knowledge we were hired to pro-vide students. This is what teaching has been about, and what we went to college to do. We are ready to deliver the most engaging and innovative methods of information transfer we can think of. It's our time in the spotlight. So, what have we been doing gen-erally with that moment when we are the "sage on the stage?"

The "NeverEnding Story" Instruction

Also known as: the lecture, or some variant thereof. This is the most common form of instruction, and we are all too familiar with it. After all, we sat through countless hours of them in college. It is our pedagogical duty to pass on the tradition to our students as well, right? Why? Thinking back on my time in college, I hated sitting through lectures. Most of us, if we are being honest with ourselves, hate them as well. It's a passive, sit-n-get activity that requires nothing on the part of the receiver other than an attention span. Attention spans that are not wired for that long, might I add, even as adults. But, we sit through our lectures in college, hours of them. High school, well, we have to prepare students for college, right? So, let's lecture. Middle school can't let the high school down, so let's lecture there, too. Primary and elementary, we know what would happen if you tried to lecture for anything over five minutes. But, we will be tested on the lecture at some point, and without that informa-tion, we cannot succeed. Lectures, use them wisely if necessary. Otherwise, are there ways students can discover this same infor-mation on their own?

The "Here, Read/Copy/Fill-in-the-Blank/Etc. This" Instruction

This is sometimes initiated along with the lecture, but has enough nuance that it is a category all on its own. This instruc-tion primarily involves receiving information through a lecture, but often through a PowerPoint presentation, reading material, instructional video, something for students to observe. This often is given in conjunction with some type of information-gathering tool for students to interact with as they observe. These could be fill-in-the-blank notes, graphic organizers, guiding questions, sentence stems, or anything for students to collect the necessary information from the presentation. While this may be a little more interactive and engaging than a lecture by way of gathering the necessary information, sometimes it ends up being a "moving the pile" type of activity. For example, students in a class take fill-in notes off a PowerPoint. The next day, the students use these notes to complete a graphic organizer. This, in turn, is used for making study cards. Are there better ways for students to interact with information rather than just moving it from place to place? Could we be asking more of their interaction with information that calls for evaluation, analysis, and critical thinking rather than copying a word from the board to a page?

The "Get to Work" Instruction

At the heart of this instruction, or lack thereof, is just handing out an assignment and telling the students, just that, to "get to work." A teacher might hand out a worksheet or workbook. If they want to get techy, the teacher might direct students to an online assignment awaiting them in their learning management system that has all the resources linked, an assignment to complete and turn in, perhaps with a little bit of online collaboration built in to shake things up a bit. Perhaps there's an online platform with all types of monitoring, regulating, and adjusting, to which students can log in, remain on for the entirety of the class time, and return the next day to do it all over again. Here's the reminder again. We cannot program our way out of subpar Tier 1 instruction. Regardless of the delivery method or how student-centered it might appear to be, this type of instruction requires nothing on the part of the teacher during class time. It may have been designed beforehand, but all is ready for students to come right in and get to work on the assignment. So the question is this, is this about the learning or is this about the work?

The "Rise of the Machines" Instruction

Finally, and closely related to the "Get to Work" instruction, is this method. Technology is an amazing thing. There is so much we can do with it to enhance the learning in our classroom. From creating, to collaborating, to researching, technology makes so many more things possible now than when I first stepped into a classroom over 20 years ago. But there's a dark side to all of our advances in this area. Some may use technology to provide the majority of the instruction for students in class. Some students come to school and work through an entire course, instruction included, while staring at a screen. Other classroom instruction is delivered time and again via YouTube videos or other online tutorials. Nothing can be streamed, programmed, or provided by a processor that can be as effective as you, a living, breathing, supportive, and knowledgeable adult in the classroom. Teachers listen, adapt, provide feedback, supply alternatives, and a million other things that we do during our instruction in class. No screen can provide this. Is it acceptable to use videos or other technology-based resources during instruction? Of course. But they need to be chosen with a specific purpose for the learning and not become the source of learning itself. Technology, just like anything else we choose for instruction, must be intentionally used for impact on learning instead of becoming instruction itself.

What Instruction Designed for Learning Looks Like

It is safe to say that there is a need for instruction in our lessons. Without instruction, students would enter learning with no guidance or purpose. They would begin to tackle whatever task was presented to them blindly. But, we want them to be prepared to show their learning off. Just like every other part in our design, the Instruction needs a purpose. We have to make those decisions ahead of time based on a few things, instead of getting up in front of the class and passing on content knowledge. That requires clarity on our part, assistance on our part, and assessment on our part to get them coached up and ready to tackle the learning. This is the true nature of instruction. It is not about pouring content knowledge into their heads, it's about preparing them for the learning that lies ahead.

Introduce the Learning Task

In the Opening, we introduced the Learning Target, or goal for the learning of the day. Now, in the Instruction, it's time to introduce the Learning Task designed from the work in Chapter 5. Remember, none of this stuff about learning should be a secret from the students. Here in the Instruction is where we want to introduce students to what is coming up in their learning. For the Work Session ahead, we have designed a Task that will clearly demonstrate the learning of the target in a way that is clear to all who participate. As we read before, this is actually where most of our students' learning will be taking place, while working through the Task. They will struggle, make mistakes, reference tools, figure things out, question, challenge thinking, and all the other cognitive processes that involve what learning really is all about. It's our job to prepare them for it.

This is why one of the key objectives for us in the Instruction is to make sure the students know what the Task coming up is. Students leave the Opening with curiosity and wonder and energy and excitement because we made purposeful choices on ways to introduce the goal for their learning today. Now, we need to tell them more about how they will get the learning accomplished and the evidence that will show everyone in the room that it happened.

The important thing to remember during the Instruction is this: make sure you make the connection to the Learning Target. Again, the target is what every single aspect of the lesson has been designed around in the first place. It is the "what we are learning." It was used to design a Task to demonstrate "why we are learning it." And soon, as part of the Instruction, the target will also drive our choices when deciding on the "how will we know we've learned it?" So, make sure when you are introducing the Task to tie it directly to the Learning Target. Without those connections, students may see the things we do in the classroom as disjointed segments of instruction and work, instead of a cohesive, everything-working-together-for-learning, design that we are wanting to provide for them.

Provide the G.I.S.T (Guided Information, Skills, and Tools)

In well-designed instruction, teachers provide the G.I.S.T. (Guided Information, Skills, and Tools) needed for the students to complete the Task for learning during the upcoming Work Session. Yes, the acronym is a pun on the word gist because what we should be providing for students is the substance or essence of what they will need, in other words, the gist. Stopping teaching does not mean we stop instruction. It is simply a mindset change. The G.I.S.T. allows us as learning engineers to take a step back, look at what we are asking as the desired results of learning in the Task, and come up with what we, in turn, must supply our learners with in order for them to be successful. This is the vital role of you being the facilitator of learning in the room. Let's look at the G.I.S.T.

Guided. This means you are the lead. You, the teacher, lead and guide students through the upcoming information and processes. Without you, our learners are just thrown things to work on without clear guidance. This is the part where direct instruction shines. Guided also means "by you." No video, technology, program, or any other resources will ever replace you as a guide through learning. Well, that is until artificial intelligence and our robot overlords finally take over. There is nothing that can do what you do. As you guide, there will be questions, challenges, discussions, and many other things students may respond with as needs of their learning. Again, nothing (yet) can do that other or better than you. But, this guidance is also meant to be concise and brief, so as to not make the lesson more about the teaching instead of learning being the main event. It is their learning after all, and we have to first guide, and then let go.

Information. What are the facts, numbers, formulas, texts, and other tangible data you must guide your learners through in order for them to take it and use it on the task to show learning? In other words, what materials do students need to interact with, gain information from, pull research out of, manipulate, or modify in some way during the Task? Relating to this, and this is a short tangent, why ask students to copy notes from a PowerPoint? Moving information from one place to another isn't learning. Could we get more authentic learning accomplished by giving students the information in the first place and designing tasks for them to manipulate, analyze, dig into, and evaluate? Is knowing the information at the recall level necessary for students to complete the Learning Task? If not, then guide them to the information and turn them loose with it to demonstrate their learning on another level. For example, instead of fill-in-the-blank or guided notes off a presentation, pass the completed notes. Now, referring to the Learning Target of "I can . . ." ask students what information they may need to collect, interact with, and analyze in order to demonstrate their learning based on the target. They now have a direction and a purpose behind interacting with information, in a collaborative process involving the sharing and evaluating of ideas and information while also giving them the content they need to move ahead with the mundane rewriting of notes. It will save you and them more time and frustration than you can imagine.

Skills. What actions and processes will you need to guide learners through so they can submit their learning to you? Do you need to model annotation, working out a linear equation, thinking aloud during your reading? What actions do your learners need to have modeled to put into practice? This all relates to the actions they will be demonstrating while they are completing the Task of the Work Session. Modeling these skills is one of the most important aspects of the G.I.S.T. The reason is that this is our chance to not only show students what is expected, it also allows us to demonstrate our thinking while working through it.

Some of the most powerful modeling moments happen when you can show your students that you have moments of struggle or moments of pause. Sometimes we have moments where we need to reach out for assistance, where we need to access a helpful tool, or where we need to stop and try another method of approach. This is what our students need to see when we guide them through the skills. They need to see what struggle in the skills looks like just as much as they need to see what success looks like. This guided practice you are modeling will eventually turn into students' individual practice of their own. We provide the guided modeling of skills to give them a realistic picture of what this looks like for learners so they can emulate and also make their practice their own.

Tools. What will you provide for the learners who get "stuck?" Where can learners turn, before running to the teacher, in order to escape their own misunderstanding and learn to move forward as owners of their own learning? On the other hand, where can learners who master the Task go to find ways to take their learning further and deeper? These are the tools we must provide for our students if we want them to truly take ownership in their learning. Tools don't only benefit the students. They are one of the ways we can take a classroom of 30 and shrink it down to a class of less than 10. Before you leave thinking you have walked into some timeshare presentation or that I'm trying to sell you a cure-all snake oil, hear me out.

A teacher's class was taking an assessment once. Looking out at the classroom, most students were fervently working, head down, figuring out solutions. However, every few minutes, a random head would lift up, turn, and stare for a split second or two at an empty space on the left wall of the classroom. Students would be lost in that stare momentarily, and then return right back to the assessment. This happened over and over again. By the time the bell rang, I had to know what was up. On my way out, as I thanked the teacher for her time, I asked, "Hey, what is up with that space on the wall over there? There were around eight of your students who stopped what they were doing to look over there at different times throughout the class."

"Oh, that's where I keep their tools for their current unit." She went on, "That space on the wall is where they find any example, anchor chart, or guidance they might need. They know to look there first." There was the answer. This class knew where to look when they needed assistance. It was so ingrained in them to look in that direction, that even when there was nothing there, they still would look. This teacher also placed the tools, references, and targets from the current unit back up on the wall after the assessment in another part of the room. Actually, her entire wall space, from one corner to another, were these materials grouped by units with connections made between all the elements, providing a map for students to reference any-time, to see where they've been and how it all connected. Pretty impactful use of some walls, right?

The point of your tools is to give students something they can work through themselves or collaboratively when they find they are stuck in a misconception, moment of struggle, or misstep in their learning. It's these tools that allow you as a teacher to facilitate learning, rather than constantly teach. Students can use flowcharts, worked examples, concept maps, any tool you have prepared for them to engage with and get out of the place they are stuck in their learning. The key in designing tools lies in pro-viding what is needed by the students for them to produce evi-dence of the learning of the day. It is more than what text they will read or problems they will solve. It is about what will they need to access, use, work through, test, evaluate with later in the Work Session to move upward in their learning.

The same is true for your students who have mastered the learning of the day. Have you provided a tool or pathway they can utilize to move beyond in their learning? Can they access additional resources, conduct different inquiries, present alter-native solutions or any pathway they can take to engage in and display deeper learning relating to the target?

These tools, along with the Success Criteria, allow the teacher to turn your students loose into learning. They know what is expected, what to anticipate, and more importantly, they know where to turn to for the *more* they might need. Our motto while working in class was "Try Three Before Me." Students knew that there were always three options to try before raising their hands for my assistance. After all, I was small grouping with students needing more intensive interventions. Students outside of this group knew to access the Success Criteria first, Tools next, then seek out peer collaboration before heading my way. This is what turning learning over to whom it belongs is about. This is how learning happens when we design it for our learners to own.

The G.I.S.T. has to be anticipated for, designed for, and planned for implementation in your classroom in order for learners to take ownership in their learning and move them-selves forward. Some of us have tried to provide this "on the fly" for our students, and it might have worked. But we have to ask, "Could they have accomplished *more* if we make intentional decisions about what they will need to tackle the upcoming learning?" This way, the majority of your class can, with little assistance on the teacher's part, take charge of their learning and manage it themselves. This leaves the teacher with the time and opportunity to take the small group of struggling learners and work more intensely to remediate.

Determine Success Criteria

One of the most important tools we provide for our students in the Instruction is the Success Criteria. As we looked at in the previous chapter, a Task should have qualities students can observe. What that means for designing learning is providing concrete, visible measures of success that a student can "see" in their work in order for them to take ownership in their learning and seek to move upward in the mastery of a Learning Target. The more tangible we can make the success of the evidence for their Tasks to be and appear to our students, the easier it is for them to identify areas of need in their learning, to target specific tools or strategies, to seek out, value, and tie feedback together with their Task and what successful evidence looks like.

Let's try something out. Go get a sheet of paper and a writing instrument. If there is someone else around, tell that person to join you in this exercise. Now, get a timer of some kind: your phone, a watch, a clock, mini hourglass from a random board game. Set your timing device, let's say you have two minutes. Once you have gathered your materials and the timer is ready for all those participating, here is your task. Your instructions are simply to draw a house. Go! Two minutes have now passed.

Let's see how you did. If you want to remain truly objective, take this book and your drawing to someone else and allow them to score your work. If you are alone, we'll use the honor code. Here is the scoring guide for your drawing of a house:

1. Give yourself 10 points for every window shown in the drawing.
2. Give yourself 30 points for a front entry door.

3. Award 15 points if you have some form of landscape feature like a tree or shrubbery.

4. You can add 30 points if your house has a chimney, but if your chimney has smoke coming out, subtract 50 points instead because fires are dangerous.

5. If you have a sun on your paper, add 50 points, but if your sun has a face on it or multiple lines coming out of it, subtract 75 points instead because that is not how the sun really looks.

6. Add 5 points each for any bird in the sky you have drawn only if they don't look like the letter "m."

7. Subtract 10 points for every cloud in the sky you have.

8. If you have a fence, add 25 points.

9. If your house is drawn in 3 dimensions, add 100 points because you are an artist.

10. Finally, if your drawing has a pet of some kind portrayed, add 20 points because animals are cute. But, if your drawn pet is a cat, subtract 40 points because I'm not a cat person.

Now, total up your score. Write your score nice and big at the top of your drawing and hang it on the fridge to show off your fine work to friends, family, or whomever will be in need of something cold to drink later. If someone else did this with you, compare your scores. How did you do? Did you get the score you anticipated or wanted? The task was pretty simple, right? Draw a house. You should have done well.

If at any moment during scoring you felt aggravated, frustrated, less than intelligent, or even downright cheated out of something, you are not alone. And if you felt this way during something like this and you are an adult, imagine what a 13-year-old feels on an assignment. Regardless of the emotional aspect of it, I bet if you knew what a successful house drawing was supposed to include and exclude before you completed your task, I am sure you would have drawn things differently.

Students in our classroom are no different. They want to do well and show what they are learning. In order to have that clarity, we must design Success Criteria and present it ahead of time to students, the more student-centered and detailed the better. If we keep what is expected of students a secret, how will they ever know where they are, where they want to go, and what they need to work on in order to get there? We owe it to their learning to make these concrete and tangible qualities known about their learning ahead of the Task. But, we also owe it to ourselves as teachers.

Teachers, if you want to turn that class of 25 students into a class of 5, you need quality Success Criteria to do it. Imagine this: you have assigned a Task to your class. Students are aware of the tools they need to access to escape any misunderstandings they come across. Others know the pathways to take when they have mastered the learning of the day. All are using the Success Criteria to self-assess and monitor where they are and where they want to go next. You now can focus on a small group to remediate with those four or five students who need additional support. This is possible only with a clear picture of what success looks like for the learning of the day, available for students to compare and contrast their own evidence with.

Success Criteria is one of the vital legs of the three-legged stool of teacher clarity. Referring to Hattie's questions from an earlier chapter (Hattie & Yates, 2009), this is the last piece of the puzzle needed for clarity to happen and get us one of the key engagement qualities of a Task, but also the 0.84 effect size teacher clarity gives us (Corwin, August 2021).

1. What am I learning? (*Learning Targets – Chapter 3*)
2. Why am I learning it? (*Relevant Task – Chapter 5*)
3. How do I know I've learned it? (*Success Criteria*)

Tasks are arguably the most important aspect of lesson design. Remember, it is in the Work Session where most of the learning happens. If teachers find they cannot develop Success Criteria for their assignments, then chances are the assignment is not worth giving because it does not really *show* learning happened. It may show that students were compliant and did as they were told, but how do we know they learned anything? That is the importance of quality Success Criteria. The realization of the potential of two years' worth of growth (0.88 effect size) comes when we have clearly defined quality work, allow students to address their needs, seek out learning, reflect, and revise with quality feedback that is tied directly to Success Criteria (Corwin, August 2021).

Assess Where They Are

This will be the last piece to consider in the Instruction designed for learning, and it is one I personally missed the mark on in the classroom for many years. As of this moment in the lesson, you have prepared students to take on the Task. You have provided an explanation and a modeling of what the Task requires, how it will help demonstrate the learning of the day, what tools to use, what pathways to take, and at this point it would be safe to say that most of us would agree that it is time to turn the students loose into the Learning Task. But, I would like to offer something for you to consider that may help inform some possible last few steps you may want to take before the Work Session begins.

Typically, we would release students to work now. Regardless of whether the Task is the same or not for everyone. Despite it being collaborative or individual. Not considering any scaffolding, differentiation, or anything else related to the Task, we would feel safe in knowing we've prepared our learners for it. However, the one thing you may not have a clear picture of when you release them into the Task is where they are in their learning as they enter.

What if you designed some sort of assessment to find out where students actually were in relation to the learning of the day before they were turned loose into the Work Session? What effect could that have? For starters, if the Task was scaffolded or differentiated in some way as we previously discussed, we could know exactly where to send students during the Work Session to engage in a Task that meets them where they are, providing the equity we need for them. If the Task isn't modified or tailored in any way, assessing where students are before the Work Session begins can allow you to form more targeted collaborative groups or small intervention groups to assist in specific ways.

Assessment doesn't have to be a formal thing at all, although it can be. You can use EdTech to administer a quick formative to collect a quick set of data to divide groups up. You can use Lexile scores from a recent measure by students. But you can also simply ask, "If you feel confident about working on X, raise a five high. If you are a little iffy, raise a three. If you feel like talking with me more about it, show me a one." This, or any variation thereof, can be a simple, informal way of taking a temperature check on the upcoming Task before release. Students will tell us exactly what they need, all we have to do is give them the opportunity. Assessment isn't about a grade all the time. Assessment is nothing more than the red pin dropped on a map. It shows where we are in learning right now. It is up to us to design what will get students through the rest of the journey. But, we can never really help anyone move forward unless we know where they are starting from to begin with.

Designed Learning Instruction Success Criteria

TABLE 6.1 The Instruction Success Criteria

THE INSTRUCTION		
Time	*The TEACHER will:*	*The STUDENT should:*
25%	• Introduce and connect the Task to the Learning Target. • Engage in discussion concerning the Learning Target. • Provide the G.I.S.T of the lesson – the guided information, skills, and tools. • Lead students in discussing/determining Success Criteria. • Provide tools and escapes for misunderstanding. • Provide pathways to accelerate. • Formatively assess before entering work time to identify student groups or needs.	• Observe the general qualities of the Task that is to come and how it ties to the Learning Target. • Participate in discussion and ask clarifying questions • Engage in guided practice with the teacher and class, locating needed information. • Assist in identifying and developing measures of success for the Learning Target. • Identify tools to escape misconceptions in learning. • Identify pathways to accelerate in learning. • Use assessment results to identify areas of specifically targeted learning.

My Top Picks for the Instruction

Direct Instruction

Don't look so shocked. I know what you are thinking. If this book is about how we should stop teaching, isn't direct instruction what teaching is and has been? Well, not really. Direct instruction is an obvious go-to for this part in the lesson design. Besides, direct instruction has an effect size of 0.59 (Corwin, August 2021), which is nearly a year and a half of potential growth. Why would we ignore that?

The problem is that many of us see direct instruction as giving directions, lecturing, or some other form of pedagogical practice that leans towards more traditional teaching. In fact, direct instruction has design in its true nature and requires a great deal of intentional, instructional decisions on the part of the teacher. What is direct instruction composed of if it is not just about giving information or directions?

According to the Visible Learning Matrix, direct instruction involves many of the predetermined design qualities we've already discussed. It "refers to instructional approaches that are structured, sequenced, and led by teachers (Corwin, August 2021)." This includes having Learning Targets, Success Criteria, an engaging learning Task, and the G.I.S.T. of the lesson. All of these require design on our part ahead of time before we ever enter the classroom. We determine what we want the outcome to be and make instructional choices resulting in students being able to realize that set outcome. Designing with the end in mind is what design is all about. So, I proudly claim that I use direct instruction in my classroom with students, and you should as well. Just as long as its purpose for learning has been accounted for and designed around.

Jigsaws

With an effect size of 1.20 (Corwin, August 2021), Jigsaws are an amazing way to get instruction accomplished with students. If you haven't ever used a Jigsaw method for instruction before, it can be summarized this way: you break a larger group of needed information into smaller groups and make students responsible for investigating the learning in that specific area. Students then return back as a collective and learn the information from each smaller group together from the individual experts. It can be accomplished in different ways.

Traditionally, students are placed in groups to gain the specific information needed, let's say four groups of four. Each group is responsible for a different set of information, for example: group one is responsible for A, group two for B, and so on. The groups dig into, critique, evaluate, collect, analyze, and synthesize their assigned mini-topic. Once groups have completed their investigations, groups split up and regroup. This time, groups are composed of a representative from each topic area so that each group contains a student from group A, B, C, and D. Now group members are free to share in their expertise of their assigned knowledge, share ideas, answer questions, and inform the other three members of the group. All take turns until the entire larger topic has now been completely covered. You can modify this any number of ways to accommodate a wide variety of topics, scenarios, or groupings. Nothing really is off-limits.

So why does this work so well? First, we have students engaging in all the higher-order thinking skills we need them to be using when interacting with information. They are the ones who are digging deep and determining what is important to pass onto their peers later. Speaking of learning from peers, that is another reason contributing to a Jigsaw's success. Peer interaction during learning, whether in the form of tutoring or assessment, brings with them a range of effect size from 0.42–0.54, all of which have the potential to accelerate learning (Corwin, August 2021). What must be clear to design ahead of time in relation to your Jigsaws is a method or procedure that students have clarity in operating in, and can leave with the desired information necessary to share with others. Expectations must be in place on how Jigsaws are conducted as well. Just like with any expectation you set in your classroom, when you see things wavering, stop and remodel, reteach and reinforce what the expectations are and what successful Jigsaws look like. If you are continuing to use more traditional methods in getting content across to students during the Instruction, I urge you to give Jigsaws a try. You, and your students, will not be disappointed.

Stations

These are related to Jigsaws in that a larger chunk of information has been divided up into smaller portions. This time, instead of students being responsible for disseminating information to their peers like in a Jigsaw, the students visit various stations to encounter and collect needed information. These stations can be designed, targeting specific information, skills, or tools for students to work in or collaborate through to gain what will be necessary to take into the upcoming Work Session.

For example, in a math class, students can work through multiple stations in order to be exposed to different methods for solving two-digit multiplication problems. One station focuses on the use of a standard algorithm, another station requires students to use a visual or manipulatives to solve this type of problem, and still another has students exposed to the Area Model to calculate this. Students can travel from station to station, gaining experiences with each method before moving onto the next. If you want to take this example to another level, add in a component asking students not only to gain experience in each station's method, but to evaluate them as well. Students can make a list of pros and cons of each method, which one is easy or difficult for them. This can be accomplished in Jigsaw just as easily as well.

Again, the only limits to stations and what they can provide to students is your imagination. Stations can help students to collect needed information, to experience the modeling of guided skills, and the previewing of upcoming tools to use during the Work Session, everything a quality G.I.S.T. provides during Instruction. Teachers can choose to facilitate the entire process during stations or perhaps manage one specific one where extra attention and guidance might be necessary. Designed well ahead of time, stations can take the bulk of the Instruction's in-class responsibility off of the teacher and place it on your learners.

Instructional G.I.S.T. Designed With Clarity in Mind. Here Comes the Close

Remember, the Instruction's primary purpose is to prepare students for the upcoming Task. We have to make sure that we've established as much clarity in the upcoming learning as possible. Students must know what the goal is for the learning of the day. They must be exposed to and guided through the information they will be responsible for knowing prior to tackling the Task. Students must be comfortable with the processes and skills the teacher has modeled with, thought aloud through, and assigned practice for relating to the Task. Finally, students have to be aware of the tools they have access to during the Task they are about to enter. Knowing where tools are located, how they are used, what additional pathways are available, and anything else that may assist them in growing in their learning to come. We've designed all these with their learning in mind, especially what success will look like for their learning. Our designed Instruction is now complete with the preparation for students in mind. All that is left now in the design process is how to close the learning of the day in a way that connects and summarizes all that took place in class today for students in a meaningful way.

Questions to Consider

1. What do you consider to be the primary purpose of Instruction? How does your purpose relate to what is discussed in this chapter? Compare and contrast the two.
2. What do you see as the most challenging part of designing the Instruction for you as the teacher in your classroom? What makes this element more challenging than the others? How can the challenge be eased?
3. How do you feel about designing Tools for students to get themselves unstuck or grow in their learning? Do you think they work? What are the potential pitfalls? What are the potential successes?

4. How often do you use Success Criteria now that allows students to monitor, self-assess, and identify their own personal needs in their learning? If you don't use them, what are some reasons why? If you do use them frequently, what methods do you use that get the best results?

5. Do you currently use some type of formal or informal assessment to see what information or skills students already know or are comfortable with during the Instruction to identify possible instructional needs during the Task? Could knowing this ahead of time help you make additional decisions for the Task to improve the learning to come?

Reference List

Corwin. (2021, August). *Visible learning Meta*^x. Retrieved September 7, 2022, from www.visiblelearningmetax.com/

Hattie, J., & Yates, G. C. R. (2009). *Visible learning and the science of how we learn*. Routledge.

7

The Closing

The Closing

Welcome to the end! Here's where we are going to make those last design decisions about the learning of the day. Students have come a long way since the beginning of class. We activated their prior knowledge and curiosity at the start, gave them all the needed information and skills, showed them how to access any tools, turned them loose to work on something that gives all of us evidence that learning happened, and all that's left to do now is choose how to wrap this all up. Sounds fairly straightforward, but without some intention and purpose on our part in design and execution, we can be missing out on opportunities for making more of our learning together.

What a Teaching Closing May Look Like Now

This segment of the lesson is the most neglected and forgotten about. It is the quintessential middle child of the lesson parts that no one seems to pay attention to or that people forget exists altogether. This is an easy thing to justify to ourselves as teachers, too. We run out of time in class, we have a lesson we feel takes more than one class meeting, or maybe we never really saw a value in how we choose to end the learning time together in the first place. Regardless of our past experiences with the Closing of

DOI: 10.4324/9781003365914-8

a lesson, there's a great deal of impact worth exploring when we move away from our current teaching habits during this time.

The "Is That the Bell Already?" Closing

We've all been there. In the middle of, or what we think is the middle of, class, students are working. We are circulating the room, checking in, and providing guidance. Then all of a sudden, we hear the long monotone drone of a school bell sounding aloud for five to seven seconds, signaling that it is now time to change classes. It's that, or you hear the hum of familiar student voices right outside your door as they have begun to line up, awaiting your door opening and your class change. We've all been caught by the class change. It is a mad rush to get everything together, students or materials moved back into their rightful place for class to be dismissed. Learning just hangs in the air with no place to go. These students leave, the next file in. We can't think about it much because now the next group is here. We can't beat ourselves up over it too much, but we can think about ways to ensure we can tap into the potential of the Closing moving forward.

The "Ticket Out the Door, but Not Much More" Closing

The tried and true Ticket Out the Door. We've all done this, or a variation thereof, over and over as our classes of students leave us. They might be in the form of a question, some type of rating, perhaps graded, perhaps not. Don't get me wrong, a ticket out the door is a method of producing an effective Closing of a lesson for learning. There are a couple of issues we run into with them though. Sometimes we give a ticket out the door as students leave; they respond, we collect, and then nothing. Students return the next class day without any reference to the ticket from the prior meeting. Responses are not discussed or related back to the learning whatsoever. Sometimes the ticket receives some sort of grade, but we have to ask ourselves, is the grade given for this ticket about completion and compliance or is it about finding out more about the learning that happened in class? Then there are times where these tickets become the only way class is being concluded, and students feel the repetitiveness, the monotony, and don't value the practice at all, resulting in lackluster and run-of-the-mill responses. If we are going to use a ticket out the door, the students need some sort of quality feedback, information, progress reporting, anything that connects their responses to the learning of the day. Without that connection, it just feels like something else they are asked to do.

The "All My Bags are Packed; I'm Ready to Go" Closing

They might not be leaving on a jet plane, but they are leaving. This was one reason why I never had a clock in my classroom, even after students begged me to get one, or after the dozens I was given as holiday or teacher-appreciation gifts. Some students watch that clock, and when it reaches a certain point close to the end of the period, they have gathered all their belongings, tidied up, and are ready to exit the room. There's nothing wrong with having the classroom back in order before leaving. There should be routines in place for this type of transition to class ending to make sure chaos is not left behind and all is ready for the next class. But this type of Closing is identical to the "Mister Rogers" Opening discussed in Chapter 4. Should there be more to what we do with our students at the end of the learning of the day than just packing up with procedures? Can learning and the learning processes of the day be reinforced, solidified, or extended in some way rather than just getting ready to leave?

The "Turn in Your Work" Closing

Chances are the Work Session has an assignment involved. Students have been hard at work showing what they know and understand for a good portion of the class period. They may have been collaborating on a task, working through a digital assignment, or writing a response in their learning. It might be that we don't want to interrupt this display of work ethic early. It might be that students need additional time to get things completed. It may be that we feel like the work is more important. Whatever the reasoning, some classes end on the habitual note of "Turn in your work as you leave." Do we need the work? Absolutely. It was important enough to assign to our students to assess where they are in their learning, and we have to get a chance to look over it ourselves before being able to provide any feedback. Again, like in the case of the Ticket Out the Door and No More, if we end the learning of the day with just collecting work and don't include any reflection on what happened today in class as it relates to the learning, we are missing out on a strong connection and opportunity. Can we establish a routine where work can be collected and still have time left in class for a Closing that is designed with learning as its purpose and not just procedure?

What a Closing Designed for Learning Looks Like

I think we all feel the stress of the clock in our classrooms, whether you have one on the wall or not. I know I have, and looking back, I have seen my own classes come to an end in each of the ways described previously. Was it easier on me as the teacher to end my classes in these ways? Sure it was. But, what I was gaining by using procedural transitions or routines, I was losing in the effective impact that a quality Closing can have on my students' learning for the day. The Closing is just like any other part of the learning we have designed already. It requires intentional decisions on our part. We have to know what we want out of the Closing and design it with that purpose in mind. Making it purposeful makes it important to the learning process. Once I made the choice, designing and using a quality, active Closing at the end of my classes became as commonplace as any other part of my lesson. Although, to be completely honest, I did have to set an alarm for each class period reminding myself that it was time for the Closing in order to make it a priority in my students' learning experiences. Their experiences in class daily, in my mind at least, are like another leg of a journey of learning. We started with a goal for today's learning, everything we've done has been designed around it, and all our actions in class have been focused on it. What better way to end today's travels in learning than to see the progress that was made, the missteps that were taken, the learning that was gained, and the plan for tomorrow? That's what the design and practice of a quality close is all about.

Engage in Summarizing the Learning of the Day

The primary goal of a Closing designed with learning in mind is to find out what learning happened during our time together in class. After all, that's the reason why we had class in the first place, right? The students have a target for the learning of the day. We've been revolving around it during the entire class period. We introduced and connected it in the Opening, gave Instruction around it, worked through a Task to measure it, and now we have one thing left to address: how far did we get today?

This can be accomplished while also providing the engaging qualities needed to get students feeling the urge to be involved. In fact, and in general, most of the methods we used to activate students' prior knowledge and engage their curiosity in the Opening can be slightly modified to become just as effective in The Closing. The focus is now not so much about what they knew *before* the learning today, but what they know *now* after experiencing the learning. Turn and talks, what-ifs, sorts, and so many others can be used to up the engagement. The only difference now is asking the question, "How do I need to modify these methods so they produce a summary of today's learning?"

What should be the focus of a summary anyway? You can always craft them around our magical three questions for clarity: what did I learn? Why did I learn it? How did I show that I learned it? We can construct our summary around conceptual knowledge gained today. We can build them around what procedures or skills we acquired to solve a problem or answer a question. We can focus them around the relevance of our learning today and summarize why that matters. We can demonstrate a summary of our collected evidence from our work, proving to all in the room learning happened. Even if we did not reach the end goal we desired today, we still can summarize where we started and where we ended up after our experience together in this one class period.

We can also use an assessment to answer this question. After all, an assessment is nothing more than a gauge displaying where students are currently. It can be informal, and I have found that some of the most effective ones are. Remember, the goal is for everyone to have a clear, overall picture of what learning occurred today. Sometimes this is completed in a more formal way, with a quiz or mini assessment. Just remember, the method used to assess must be chosen for a purpose as well. If I really want to know if my students learned something, what's the best way

I can collect that summary data that gives us a true image of what they really know and can do? More on assessments in Chapter 8.

Reflect on the Process

Part of the process in discovering what learning occurred today should involve some sort of reflection on the part of the students. Looking back at the totality of the learning experiences today, from the Opening to the Instruction to the Work Session and now in the Closing, students need to examine what happened. Our job in designing the Closing is this: we need to provide the lens through which students look back so that they see what we want and what they need to see relating to their learning. Since we've discovered most of the learning takes place while they are working through the Task, it only makes sense we steer students' sights to the process in which they participated today. Specifically, we want them to reflect on two things: the successes and the slip-ups – but we also have a part to play in this, and that's about praise.

Successes

What better way to wrap up the learning of the day than to discover with each other what actually worked? Identifying areas of success in our learning today is not about figuring out who got this right or who got that right. Reflection during this time has a different and more important priority. Our mission now when it comes to reflecting on the successes of the day is about *what* worked well to advance our learning and *why* it worked so well.

"Who discovered something today that really helped you during your learning?" "Who wants to give a fellow student a shout-out for using a strategy that ended up helping you learn today?" "What about this method worked so well with what you were learning today?" These are the questions we need to be discussing and sharing, surrounding success. Here's an opportunity to discover something, that as an adult you may have never considered having an effect on your students' learning. We can be learning from the students and should be. Once we discover those success makers, we can record them, display them, make them into a tool or a worked example, and have them to use moving forward for student use and self-help.

Slip-Ups

I would argue that these need and deserve more attention and celebration during, and also at the end of, our learning time with students. The reason is because we learn from our mistakes, missteps, and misunderstandings more than when we get something "right." Other than during individual feedback during the Work Session, there's no better time than in the Closing to air and address where our learning might have slipped off the tracks today.

It doesn't have to be anything complicated. It can be as simple as, "Who got frustrated today while you were learning?" Notice, I didn't ask anyone about any mistakes they might have made. Asking about frustrations, aggravations, or times of downright tantrums can bring some of the areas of struggle to light. Once we know what those moments are, we can collaborate together about how individuals worked through them, what strategies they used, what tools they accessed, and how they grew in their learning as a result. If we want to narrow the focus and still have students feel safe and comfortable with sharing their slip-ups, we can ask, "Did anyone notice some things in your learning today that could have led a fellow classmate to make a misstep?" We aren't focused on the mistake, we aren't even addressing who might have made a mistake. What we want to know through our sharing here in the Closing is what might have or did cause the mistake. Now we can collaborate together, identifying any preparations or fixes that will help avoid those same types of missteps from happening in the future.

Praise Pitfalls and Progress

If there is something I could recommend to change the learning culture of any classroom, it would be to foster a routine of praise. It's easy to praise the successes we discussed previously. It's in our nature as teachers to want to recognize moments like this in our students. It's why we bought all those stamps and stickers to put on their papers after all, right?

So, while we easily and oftentimes almost unintentionally celebrate the successes, we have to make a point to praise the pitfalls. You know what I would love to see invented for the classroom? I would like a big red buzzer, button, or plunger like you see on game shows and other competitions. What I would like to see is this in place in a classroom, and whenever students make or discover a mistake or pitfall, they run over and hit the buzzer. A loud air horn type of sound blares, confetti shoots out of the ceiling corners of the room, and we all get to cheer because someone has made a mistake! So, maybe the confetti is a step too far, but I can see the other being a reality. And it should, we should be praising the mistake for making us aware of something we didn't know about before. We should be thanking the one who made the mistake. We should be celebrating and making these students part of our Learner's Hall of Fame in our room.

We should also be praising the progress we made today in our learning. Coming together at the end of the learning time should be about the good we did, the bad we discovered, and the distance we traveled toward our learning goal for today. Remember, the Closing, like everything else we designed for in the learning today, points to the end goal of the Learning Target. Did we meet it? Did we go past it? Are we coming up short? Where are we going tomorrow as a result? Praise and establishing a culture of its continual use, especially in the Closing, may help students see what this learning thing really is about more clearly and move forward with more intentional purpose.

Designed Learning Closing Success Criteria

TABLE 7.1 The Closing Success Criteria

THE CLOSING		
Time	*The TEACHER will:*	*The STUDENT should:*
15%	• Formally or informally assess student understanding of the Learning Target. • Provide feedback for any common misconceptions in understanding. • Summarize and praise progress toward the Learning Target. • Connect today's learning with where previous learning was and where future learning will be going.	• Share and justify learning using language of the standard. • Ask any lingering clarifying questions about the Learning Target. • Reflect on the Learning Target and provide evidence of progress based on the Work Session product. • Recognize the link between previous learning and today's learning while anticipating the learning to come.

Top Picks for the Closing

Thought, Sought, and Ought Closing

Here's a Closing that teachers can change up each time it is used. There's actually six different combinations you can try when using these. It is a great way to incorporate many of the elements a quality Closing should address. We are focusing on summarizing the learning through the thoughts we had prior to, during, or after learning. This method also has students reflecting on what they intended to seek out or discovered that they needed to find while learning. Lastly, the students can address any missteps or misconceptions about today's learning, or even plan out where they would like to take learning next. Here's how they work:

1. *Thought* – This should be about exactly that, the thoughts students had before, during, or after learning. They typically center on the content and information. These questions can be used as feedback for you about the content in the Instruction or the processes in the Task. These thoughts can focus on students' opinions concerning how far we got in learning today. They can be centered around students' thoughts in reaction to what they sought or things they found they ought to do. It all depends on the purpose you have for the end result.

2. *Sought* – This addresses the things students decided to look for today during their learning. The seeking during learning revolves around the process or actions we took today. What information did they think was worthy to go search for? What skill or tools did they seek out? Did what they thought lead them to what they sought? Or did the mistakes they ought to be aware of lead to seeking out assistance? And what learning will be sought next?

3. *Ought* – I love these because they force a moment of reflection about the learning process of the day. This has students predicting or reflecting, depending on how it's used. What do students think ought to be the first steps of the learning that happened today? What ought to be

our next steps tomorrow? When following the sought or thought, the ought can identify common pitfalls that other students ought to avoid or mistakes that individual students recognized and corrected during learning.

Some examples:
Elementary Life Science

Thought – What did you think about or already know about sharks before learning today?
Sought – What information did you look for and find about sharks?
Ought – What is something else we ought to do tomorrow as we learn more about sharks?

Or . . .

High School Algebra

Ought – What missteps did you make and what ought others do to avoid them?
Sought – What tools or methods did you seek out to help you in those missteps in solving two-step equations?
Thought – After your search and mistakes, what important steps do you plan to think about while solving two-step questions in the future?

Again, tailor the order and the questions to whatever are your desired outcome for students' summary of learning as well as their self-analysis and feedback about the process. These can make for some meaningful discussions around what worked and what didn't work today in class. They can drive our work moving forward into what the class should do tomorrow in response to today. And they can help summarize our progress and conceptual thinking about the day's learning. Give them a try, change them up, mix and match, and see what results you get from students expressing their thoughts, soughts, and oughts.

Necessary Nine Closing

This one is pretty simple. It allows for individual responses, collaboration, or a mixture of both. Students have 90 seconds to write down the "Necessary Nine" key words they would need to be able to explain the learning of the day to someone else. Remember, learning isn't only about the content knowledge or information. It's also about the process and the progress.

Students make a quick list of nine words on a Post-It note or paper. Then, they must find someone else in the room, and they must have a conversation about today's learning. This conversation must include the Necessary Nine they have written down. Students share their summaries, mistakes, missteps, successes, confusions, and solutions with each other. You can have your students report out, sharing not only what they wrote down themselves, but what great ideas and feedback they received from their peers they interacted with.

Feel free to adjust the number of words that you deem necessary based on the grade level you teach. I am sure a third-grade class may benefit from having their Closing revolve around a set of Fantastic Four terms. Whatever you choose to do, remember to modify what you use for the desired outcome for the quality Closing you want your students to participate in through their summarizing of their learning journey today.

Drawing the Journey Closing

This one allows for a lot of creativity on the students' part when it comes to their artistic sides. The premise is this: if you had to draw a map that shows your learning journey today, what would it look like? Students are free to respond in a number of ways.

Students can draw a landscape, complete with mountains, rivers, valleys, canyons, bears, scorpions, or ill-tempered squirrels. These illustrations are designed to show where students started in their learning, the successes they had during the journey like discovering something new, the pitfalls they had, wrong turns they made, and eventual arrival at their destination. They can be represented as treasure maps, vacation guides, or anything dealing with traveling from one place to another. You can give students complete control in what they draw to represent certain things, or you can assign specific images to certain parts of their journey. Students can annotate their maps with statements or sentences citing the learning of the day. Make these whatever you like. For older students, this can easily be turned into a Google Maps journey detailing the turns that required "recalculating," or the places that the GPS took them on a faster route in their journey.

Basically with this Closing, you are still addressing all the great things a Closing can provide in the way of identifying the summary, wrong turns, achievements, and final destination. This gives students a chance to visually represent this analogy in an engaging way to share visually with others in the room on the same journey.

With This Learning at the Close, There Is Still More to Come

You have reached the end of the design process for today's learning for your classroom. You have made intentional choices based on what provokes and promotes learning in our students. All that is left to do is to put this design into action. Will every design you create be a complete success? Was every lesson plan you made previously? The difference is now you have focused your attention on what is required for learning to happen in the room, and not just teaching to take place. You have designed with an end in mind, the end being the highest quality and most impact-filled experience possible for your students. You may be wrapping this design up in the choice of Close, but today's learning only seeks to inform your designs for tomorrow. With design in mind, the next chapter contains a variety of information relating to our time together through this book. I hope you find its contents helpful as it provides some materials, methods, and mechanisms that may make your personal journey into designing learning a little easier.

Questions to Consider

1. Do you see a value in what could happen in the Closing after reading this chapter? What do you see? What do you question?
2. Do you have a practice currently in place that you use to close the learning of the day with your students before they leave? Is it giving you the information you want or need about students and their learning?
3. Is there a practice of identifying and collecting mistakes and missteps students make? How could you turn this practice into a tool for your students?
4. How much do you praise the things that are happening in your classroom for learning that are *not* about just having the right answer? Could you see this being a motivator for your students or a culture that could affect learning?
5. What is the biggest challenge you face in implementing a quality Closing in each of your lesson designs? What can be done to help make them happen on a more consistent basis?

8

Tips, Tools, and Templates

Purpose for This Chapter

While the book chapters themselves provide reasoning, discourse, and guidance behind the questions and decisions made behind the designing of learning rather than the traditional teaching we have been doing, I wanted to provide some additional resources here for learning engineers to use as a jumping-off point into their journey into design. Some of the materials housed here are just overall simple suggestions, some are more meticulous methods, and others are specifically refined tools for your modification, manipulation, and use in your own classrooms as you start thinking about how to design the most effective learning opportunities possible for the students you serve. I hope you will take these, get creative, and make them your own to best serve the students you provide learning for in your room.

Chapter 2 – Teacher and Student Mindset: Tips

Ten Tips That Help Build Positive Teacher/Student Relationships

1. <u>Take care of yourself first</u> – Your well-being comes first. You can't take care of others without taking care of your needs first. I know this is a difficult one for teachers, as we tend to be a selfless bunch. We have to be well, be

DOI: 10.4324/9781003365914-9

happy, and be present so that our students see and feel the same in our classrooms as well.

2. <u>Believe in every single kid</u> – While a lot of the actions on this list can be observed from the outside, this one is more of an internal task. We must believe in each and every one of our students. The second we believe any less, then we start expecting less. This is where the seed of inequity gets planted. Every student can and every student will if two things happen: we believe in them and we do whatever it take to support them.

3. <u>Know and call all students by their preferred name</u> – This may sound ridiculous, but so much depends upon something this simple. It costs us nothing, and it might mean everything to them.

4. <u>Get to know all of your students</u> – This is especially true for those students who make the classroom experience a bit more challenging for you as a teacher. Try the 2 x 10 strategy Lisa Kitzmann introduced (McKibben, 2014). Choose to spend 2 minutes a day for 10 days in a row in conversation with a student about anything as long as it is *not* about academics. Part of teacher credibility lies in the ability to be trusted.

5. <u>They are all your favorites</u> – We all know kids pick up on things. Their radars are finely tuned instruments that can detect so many things we don't even think about like the new outfit you are wearing or the haircut you got over the weekend. They also know when there's different treatment happening. I've had many students ask me over the years if they were my favorite students and my answer was always the same. Yes, you are all my favorites.

6. <u>Greet students at the door</u> – Not with just a "Good Morning," but something specific and genuine. Knowing your students makes this much easier. Handshakes, fist bumps, high-fives, hugs are also welcoming gestures. They need to know you are happy to see them and that their being at school today is important to you.

7. <u>Transform class rules</u> – Instead of class rules, try this at the beginning of the term with students. Discuss what learning is, what it looks like, what it requires out of everyone, and write down the shared beliefs and values everyone shares when it comes to what happens in the classroom as far as learning is concerned. Now, collectively write the expectations students have for each other as it relates to what they believe and value about learning. Now you have a set of agreed-upon expectations that everyone holds each other accountable to. Next, ask students what their expectations of you as their teacher are. Making students part of the process in what behaviors are expected in the classroom builds a collective culture.

8. <u>Treat students as the kids they are</u> – Whether they are 8 or 18, our students are not shrunken adults. We shouldn't expect them to be in their thoughts, actions, or attitudes. We also shouldn't expect them to show up knowing the expectations of the classroom or school. Just like with math, science, or reading, these have to be learned like everything else.

9. <u>Make contact with those at home</u> – We want our students on our team. The learning team. If students don't like you, chances are they won't work for you or with you on that team. That's why we want to nurture and nourish these positive relationships with them as much as possible. We also need another very important member to join up on the team: someone from home. Making contact with those at home will only help strengthen this team and make for a successful season. Sure, we need to contact home when there are issues involving something detrimental to learning such as behaviors, grades, or absences. But if you really want a strong team, make it a habit of contacting home on things going well and successes in learning.

10. <u>Listen first</u> – See that student over there in the far left row with his head down. Our first instinct is to bark a command at him to get his head up and pay attention. There's a whole lot of reasons why that head might be

down in the first place. Instead of jumping right into addressing a compliance issue with commands and demands, try asking about what's going on and listening with genuine concern. A listening adult just might be what that kid with his head down today needs the most.

How to Stop and Collaborate. Just Listen to These Three Ways

1. Get involved in a Professional Learning Community (PLC) – The concept has been around for decades, but if we really want to change what is happening in the classroom for our learners and ourselves, it will take a team. That's where PLCs come into play. There's so much out there about forming them, working in them, and making them productive. You may have had a lackluster experience in the past with PLCs. I know I have. It might have been your PLC was a micromanaged process that was more about compliance on a form or in a meeting rather than getting actual work done. Or, on the other end of the spectrum, the PLC you were in was more about complacency, just meeting to talk about things that really didn't have an effect on learning. Whatever your experience has been, I encourage you to give it another go. Find resources and dig into the real work of PLCs, which is learning by the way. You can always bring this book along and make that a starting point for instructional conversations. Whatever you do, share the experience, the expertise, and the energy with the other educators in your building.

2. What about singletons? – There are teachers out there who are silos, not by choice, but by circumstance. Some of you are high school teachers with a specific content-area course like no one else in the building, while others of you are the one elementary music teacher in your school or district. If you are a singleton, there is good news. We have the Internet. No longer do you have to be alone. We are connected more now than ever before. This means you can reach out to fellow teachers in your district who are teaching similar content, and have virtual PLCs or discussions surrounding designing learning for

your respective rooms. If you are alone in your district, reach out to surrounding districts for someone like yourself in need of collaboration. We all need each other in this profession. There's no excuse not to help make each other better and collaborate to improve learning for our students.

3. <u>Get online</u> – If 1 and 2 aren't an option for whatever reason, here's one that is accessible to all and a source of endless pedagogical wealth and wisdom. First, chances are your state has online resources in the forms of training, videos, or other guidance you can pilfer through for materials and resources as well as groups to follow or newsletters to subscribe to. If that doesn't work, go check out some of the major educational world's heavy hitters when it comes to professional development. Find just about any publisher of books about teaching or education, go to their website and you will, more often than not, find webinars, videos, and discussion boards to become involved with. There is not a month that goes by that I am not signed up for a free webinar from one or more companies. Last of all, get on social media. There is a great community of educators out there who are sharing and seeking ways to improve what we do for our students in the classroom. I suggest choosing wisely because there are those online who want to focus their attention and attacks on things that might not benefit you or your students. But you will have little trouble finding folks to follow who are willing to share, ask questions, and lift each other up in our profession. If you don't know where to start, here's a freebie. Find me on Twitter @letsquitteachin and I'll be happy to provide avenues to follow for more information.

Making Student Mindsets Matter

1. <u>Students need to know what we know about learning</u> – Before we ever get into anything really content-heavy, we need to make sure students know everything we know about learning. What I mean by this is students ought

to be let in on the secrets we never bother to share with them in the first place. We have them come into class and engage in a strategy that activates their prior knowledge. We know that. Do they? Should they? Why not? We should share the purposes and promises behind all the practices we put out into our classrooms for students. They should know what an Opening is for, what Instruction's purpose is, what a Task is designed for, and what a Closing strategy's goal is. It will only strengthen the culture in your classroom you are seeking to create. One that has all things pointing to learning.

2. Students need opportunities for ownership – If students know what all this learning stuff is supposed to be about, it's now time to give it over to them. We need to make sure they know whose learning it is and how they can take control and commitment over it. One practice I always loved was student-led conferences. Students kept artifacts and reflections on their learning all year long, from the very beginning. Not only did they have evidence and goals from their academic work and test scores, they also collected information about personal things related to dreams outside of the school building. When we had conferences, the students did all the talking, presenting their work, goals, and plans, and let their adult know how they can take part in supporting them in what they needed. This and so many other opportunities should be available for students to take on their learning. Most of the time, it is just a matter of us designing the opportunity for them to do so.

3. Students need self-regulatory assistance – With this newfound ownership will come frustrations. Many of our students come to us without the necessary skill sets to manage obstacles and setbacks when they occur. When students come face to face with situations they have trouble tackling, we must be ready in these moments to provide them with the tools they need. Instead of blowing up in frustration or shutting down in defeat, we have to show students what to do. So often, students

are not aware of what emotions they are experiencing, much less how to process them. When that happens, anger tends to be the final result. Teaching students how to self-regulate during learning is key. What do I do when I start to feel frustrated? What are ways I can calm down and focus? What are my escapes? Where can I turn? All of these questions and more are necessary to answer for our students, so they can become more independent and resilient learners in our rooms.

4. Students need collaborative guidance – Just as students need guidance in their individual journeys in learning, we also need to make sure students know what collaborations looks like and feels like as well. Students love working together, so do we. There are times when this works well; there are other times when it almost leads to bloodshed. Again, we have to teach this and instill this in our learners. Students have to know what it takes for quality collaboration to occur. They need guidance on how to listen and respond respectfully with others in class so that everyone can achieve great things in their learning today. It does not happen on its own. It requires guidance, boundaries, purpose, modeling, and continual practice to occur and be meaningful.

Chapter 3 – Design Framework and Learning Targets: Tools

Below in Table 8.1 is the Design Framework in its totality, detailing the four main segments of a lesson design as well as what the teacher will be doing during this time, along with what the students should be doing in reaction. Please make note of the superscript numbers throughout the framework denoting the potential effect size built into the design (Corwin, August 2021). We *have* to design for learning, knowing we have put these high-impact practices in place in order to observe and experience the success.

TABLE 8.1 Design for Learning Framework[1]

THE OPENING		
Time	*The TEACHER will:*	*The STUDENT should:*
10%	• Engage students' curiosity/involvement[2] • Activate prior knowledge around the learning[3] • Preview knowledge (if necessary) • Tie opening activity to the Learning Target[4]	• Engage in opening activity • Access prior knowledge about the learning • Gain necessary prerequisite knowledge or skills • Recognize the goal of the Learning Target
THE INSTRUCTION		
Time	*The TEACHER will:*	*The STUDENT should:*
25%	• Introduce and connect the Task to the Learning Target. • Engage in discussion concerning the Learning Target.[5] • Provide the G.I.S.T of the lesson – the guided information, skills, and tools[6]. • Lead students in discussing/determining Success Criteria.[7] • Provide tools and escapes for misunderstanding.[8] • Provide pathways to accelerate. • Formatively assess before entering work time to identify student groups or needs.[9]	• Observe the general qualities of the Task that is to come and how it ties to the Learning Target. • Participate in discussion and ask clarifying questions • Engage in guided practice with the teacher class, locating needed information. • Assist in identifying and developing measures of success for the Learning Target. • Identify tools to escape misconceptions in learning. • Identify pathways to accelerate in learning. • Use assessment results to identify areas of specifically targeted learning.

TABLE 8.1 (Cont.)

THE WORK SESSION		
Time	*The TEACHER will:*	*The STUDENT should:*
50%	• Facilitate the independent or group work on the Task.[10] • Purposefully assign collaborative groups and differentiated Tasks based on formative assessment from Instruction[11] • Monitor, assess, and document student performance • Redirect students to tools to escape and pathways to accelerate • Allow students to struggle, make mistakes, and conduct error analysis • Conference with students. • Provide standard-based feedback referring to established success criteria and Learning Target[15]	• Engage in independent or collaborative learning on the Task. • Demonstrate proficiency in skills and concepts related to the Learning Target. • Self-assess using success criteria and explain progress using standards-based vocabulary.[12] • Utilize tools to escape and pathways to accelerate.[13] • Struggle, make mistakes, determine course of action in learning and analyze errors.[14] • Conference with the teacher to receive feedback tied to the Learning Target and Success Criteria. • React to feedback, make adjustments, reflect on learning, and progress to target.
THE CLOSING[16]		
Time	*The TEACHER will:*	*The STUDENT should:*
15%	• Formally or informally assess student understanding of the Learning Target. • Provide feedback for any common misconceptions in understanding • Summarize and praise progress toward the Learning Target. • Connect today's learning with where previous learning was and where future learning will be going.	• Share and justify learning using language of the standard. • Ask any lingering clarifying questions about Learning Target. • Reflect on the Learning Target and provide evidence of progress based on the Work Session product. • Recognize the link between previous learning and today's learning while anticipating the learning to come.

[1] Collective Teacher Efficacy – 1.36 effect size – Teachers sharing the same beliefs and seeing the results from their impact using design.
[2] Curiosity – 0.90 effect size

[3] Strategies to Integrate with Prior Knowledge – 0.93 effect size

[4] Clear Goal Intentions – 0.51 effect size

[5] Class Discussion – 0.82

[6] Explicit Teaching Strategies – 0.57 size, Direct Instruction – 0.59 effect size, and many more possibilities with potential to accelerate.

[7] Success Criteria – 0.88 effect size, Teacher Clarity – 0.84

[8] Advanced Organizers – 0.42 effect size

[9] Formative Evaluation – 0.40 effect size

[10] Collaborative Learning – 0.39 effect size

[11] Differientiation – 0.46 effect size

[12] Self-Reported Grades – 1.33 effect size

[13] Strategy Monitoring – 0.58 effect size

[14] Self-Regulation Strategies – 0.54 effect size

[15] Feedback – 0.62 effect size, Feedback (Reinforcement & Cues) – 0.92 effect size, Feedback (Tasks & Processes) – 0.64 effect size

[16] The Closing reinforces many of the methods of impact used throughout the design

Learning Targets

If I had to choose the starting point for the work we do in designing learning, this would be it. We cannot make any of the other decisions we need to make for the learning we want to happen in our classrooms if we cannot first identify quality Learning Targets based on the standards. Standards are, after all, what we are supposed to teach. How we teach them is what the rest of the design process is all about. But we first have to begin with the end in mind. Perhaps the most important part of this process is actually doing the work. Sure, you can probably find a list of targets out there somewhere. Trust me, the knowledge, experience, and clarity you will gain about what you need to teach lies in taking a long, hard look at these yourself and discovering their meaning. You can use the tool in Table 8.2 to aid you in this task. Table 8.3 contains a completed example for you to reference.

TABLE 8.2 Learning Target Generator Tool

Step 1: List the chosen Standard
Write the standard you wish to unpack or deconstruct.

Step 2: Locate the "Key Words" from the Standards (i.e. VERBS and NOUNS) and translate into *Student-Friendly* Language.
Identify all the nouns and verbs directly written in the standard. Define them using student-friendly language.

Step 3: Determine what a student needs to be able to KNOW and DO to demonstrate mastery.	
What Students Need to <u>KNOW</u> (Information and Concepts)	**What Students Need to <u>DO</u> (Actions and Skills)**
Looking at the list of nouns in Step 2, list the information, concepts, and content knowledge necessary to attain mastery of this standard.	Looking at the list of verbs in Step 2, list the skills, processes and actions necessary to attain mastery of this standard.

Step 4: Looking at the results of Step 3, what are the LEARNING TARGETS (written in an "I can . . ." statement) students need as goals for their learning to show they mastered this standard?
Take the information from Step 3 and compose your Learning Targets here.

TABLE 8.3 Learning Target Generator Example

Step 1: List the chosen Standard
CCSS.ELA-LITERACY.RL.9–10.1: Cite strong and thorough textual evidence to support analysis of what the text says explicitly as well as inferences drawn from the text.

Step 2: Locate the "Key Words" from the Standards (i.e. VERBS and NOUNS) and translate into *Student-Friendly* Language.
<ul><li>cite – show where the information discussed is coming from in another text</li><li>textual evidence – information from the text that helps explain an opinion</li><li>support – help or assist</li><li>analysis – breaking something into its parts and how each part works alone and together</li><li>inferences – an opinion based on facts and evidence</li><li>drawn – taken from</li></ul>

Step 3: Determine what a student needs to be able to KNOW and DO to demonstrate mastery.

What Students Need to **KNOW** (Information and Concepts)	What Students Need to **DO** (Actions and Skills)
<ul><li>The difference between strong and weak evidence.</li><li>The concept of thorough evidence.</li><li>When to paraphrase and when to directly quote.</li><li>The difference between a fact and opinion.</li></ul>	<ul><li>Paraphrase a text</li><li>Cite information from a text</li><li>Infer based on textual evidence</li><li>Analyze a text and its features</li></ul>

Step 4: Looking at the results of Step 3, what are the LEARNING TARGETS (written in an "I can . . ." statement) students need as goals for their learning to show they mastered this standard?
<ul><li>I can break a text down into its parts and explain their purposes.</li><li>I can use information from the text to explain my ideas.</li><li>I can cite where I used information from a text.</li><li>I can make inferences about information taken from the text and support them with strong text evidence.</li></ul>

Chapter 4 – The Opening: Examples

Additional Effective Strategies for the Opening

Remember, anything can be an effective strategy for the Opening as long as it engages prior knowledge and engages curiosity. You do not have to become a master of all of them. But, choose three to five to keep in your toolbox to use every day. Again, every single day's learning needs an Opening, even if it relates back to the progress of the learning from the day before. Use these first energy-filled minutes to your advantage in the learning of the day. In Table 8.4 are 15 more ways you can open a lesson. Some can be written, others are spoken aloud, many can be both. But whatever you choose, choose what works best for your class and the learning in your room.

TABLE 8.4 Strategies for the Opening

Strategy	Method
3–2–1	List 3 things you already know about today's learning, 2 things you want to learn more about, and 1 question related to the learning.
Admit Ticket	Ask students a question as admission to class; it can be concerning prior knowledge related to the learning, learning from the prior day's lesson, or some information steering student thinking prior to learning.
Alphabet Response	Pose a topic or a question about today's learning. Students list all the words, knowledge or vocabulary they already associate with the learning beginning with letters A–Z.
Anticipation Activity	Provide students with statements about today's learning. Students can respond with how they feel about this learning or if they agree or disagree or some other qualifying response. These same statements can be used *after* learning as a summarizing or feedback tool as well.
Carousel Brainstorming	Chart paper with questions or statements from the teacher are posted around the room. Groups of students respond with thoughts on the chart paper, then rotate to another post. Students can read other responses and respond in return.
Gallery Walk	Present information, text, pictures, etc., around the room. Students walk, observing material, and responding via predetermined criteria.
Game On!	Questions or tasks related to the learning are presented as a game or competition to students.
Illustrate It	Take a concept, idea, process, or anything related to today's learning and have students draw a representation of it.
Imaginary Scenario	Students enter the room and are immediately assigned a scenario related to the learning of the day. In science, "You are all electrical engineers hired to determine the best way to provide lights to our city." ELA, "You are movie critics charged with writing the best critical analysis of an exciting scene." Math, "You work for a candy-bar company and are assigned to come up with the best packing for the newest candy bars." Students must brainstorm all they think they will need to know and learn relating to their imaginary roles.

TABLE 8.4 (Cont.)

Strategy	Method
Pass the Note	Write a question concerning today's learning on one or more sheets of paper. Pass the paper(s) to students. Students respond to the question and write another original question as well. The paper(s) continue to circulate until all students have had a chance to respond.
Post-It Questions	Students write questions on a Post-It note relating to the learning of the day and stick it to the board. Students return to their Post-Its at the end of the learning, turn it over, and compose an answer as a summarizer.
Thumbs Up/ Thumbs Down	Ask students a series of questions relating to today's learning. Students respond with a thumbs up or down to indicate their comfortability with the information or concept.
Video Clip	Find a video clip relating to the learning of the day. Students cannot simply just watch. Have them respond, evaluate, question, elaborate on the content in some way.
What's Missing?	Compose sentences about today's learning with key words or ideas left blank. Have students write or discuss the possible missing pieces.
Why, Why, and Why	Students are given a single word topic relating to today's learning. In response, they have to compose as many questions as they can. The only rule is that the questions all have to begin with the word, "why."

Chapter 5 – The Work Session: Design Tools, Feedback Tips, and More

Designing a Learning Task that is engaging can be a challenge for many of us. The template in Table 8.5 can help jumpstart the process by narrowing our focus on first identifying what Learning Target we are seeking to provide as the goal for today's learning. Our next decision must center around the question of what to provide students that results in some tangible, observable evidence that learning happened as the goal or target intended. Remember, we want the Task to result in quality evidence that is clear to all, the students and the teacher. This evidence of learning has to meet the level of the target you have set as well. In other words, the Task shouldn't require students to *identify* when the target you constructed based on the standard asks them to *analyze*. Making sure the challenge matching the level of the standard is present in the Task we are asking students to complete is a primary focus. This, along with providing as many engaging qualities as we can, helps build a quality Task displaying learning and one in which students are likely to participate during class. Feel free to combine the information from Tables 8.5 and 8.7 to create a more comprehensive design template as well to help guide you in your design process.

TABLE 8.5 The Learning Task Generator

Learning Target					
I can . . .					
The Task					
The students will . . . What is the Task that I am asking students to complete to show evidence they have met the Learning Target?					
Engaging Design Qualities Incorporated in the Task (3 minimum for Engagement)					
	Clarity		Collaboration		Novelty
	Safety		Choice		Authenticity
	Sense of Audience		Personal Response		Other:

Engagement Questions to Drive Design

We also want to provide challenging work, but we also want students to feel that urge to become involved in it as well. Table 8.6 is based on the work of Antonetti and Garver, referenced in Chapter 5. Use this set of guiding design questions to help incorporate what their research concludes as elements encouraging engagement we should strive to include in the Tasks we assign for students.

TABLE 8.6 What Makes a Task Engaging?

Quality	Definition	Design Questions to Ask
Clarity	Students know what the goal for learning is, and what success looks like.	Do students know the learning target and success criteria associated with this task for learning?
Safety	Students feel good about taking risks, making mistakes, and having different answers during learning.	How can the classroom culture and student interaction expectations be tailored to make students feel safe to take risks and make mistakes during the learning task?
Sense of Audience	Students know who will be observing their learning.	Who will be a valued audience for the product of this learning task?
Collaboration	Students have opportunities to share, learn, and work with other students.	How will students share ideas, explain, evaluate, reflect, and revise together during the learning task?
Choice	Students have choices in how to collect information and/or demonstrate their learning.	Are there multiple ways students can choose to demonstrate their learning in the task?
Personal Response	Students can react with individual thoughts in learning.	Can students bring their own life experiences and individual ideas into their responses in the learning task?
Novelty	Students' curiosity is engaged through the process and products of learning because they are seen as new or unique.	How can the learning task be designed to be fun, strange, out-of-the-box to get students excited?
Authenticity	Students see the relevance and real-world purpose behind the learning.	How can the learning task be designed to incorporate real-world and meaningful connections?

Source: Antonetti and Garver (2015)

Feedback Tips

Feedback is a vital tool in the learning happening in your classroom. Without it, students simply are just doing work for completion and compliance rather than for growth and learning. Looking back at what happens in the classroom as far as feedback is concerned, you typically find two methods dominating the rest. Surface level praise/pejorative OR a grade on a paper. If we want to see learning happen in our room, intentionally designed-for learning that occurs at high levels, we have to look at what we are providing as feedback for our students. Here are some tips to keep in mind when considering the feedback provided in your classroom.

1. Feedback requires a Learning Target and Success Criteria: Students must know the learning goal of the day and what successful evidence of that learning looks like before you can ever provide guidance leading them from where they are now to where they need to go (Hattie & Clarke, 2018).

2. Start feedback with where they are: Meeting students where they are in their learning is key. Taking their prior and current knowledge into account is the start of their journey in learning. Feedback should build up, coach up, lift up from there to guide students to the next steps. It needs to be specific and clearly understood, from start to finish, in order to be effective in improving learning (Hattie & Clarke, 2018).

3. You need to be trusted for feedback to work: Remember all the emphasis on relationships we've read about? This is another reason why they are so important. Students have to believe you have their backs and best interest at heart when you give your guidance. Otherwise, they are hesitant and reluctant to take the leap into learning you are asking of them.

4. Feedback with predestined purpose: Design the methods for your feedback with their end purpose in mind. In other words, what is a student seeking this feedback for? For example, your method of asking for receiving feedback

for learning as it relates to a process might look differently if the learning was related to a concept. How you check in and ask for feedback may need to be adjusted for clarity and usability.

5. <u>Feedback is part of the formative learning process</u>: This is why that grade on the last unit test isn't really feedback for students. That summative grade is more feedback for you, the teacher, relating to how well learning was designed for and provided, and where you need to go next in learning. Feedback lives in the formative realm for our students. They are still in the learning process, forming the connections, corrections, and correlations needed to reach the learning goal.

6. <u>Make mistakes meaningful</u>: When providing feedback, make the mistakes mean something besides the stigma of a "wrong answer." Mistakes are the only way we learn. Providing feedback in ways that remove those negative associations while tying the celebrations of next steps in learning can help create a new culture and purpose with feedback.

7. <u>Peer feedback:</u> If designed for and held to expectations, student-to-student feedback can be beneficial in the classroom. Using conversation stems and response guides to help students navigate receiving and providing feedback allows students to experience other perspectives while seeking to master today's learning.

8. <u>Listen, understand, and try:</u> Feedback only works when these three things happen. Students first have to listen and receive feedback. They have to be in a place of safety and trust, they have to value what will be given and open to hearing it out. Students also have to understand what the feedback is calling them to put into action. They must know explicitly the reasoning behind the feedback given, its potential outcome, and how to move forward in the process. Finally, they have to take the leap and act on the feedback. Once these three actions are concluded, the feedback process can start anew by reflecting on the progress made and the location now in learning.

Some Thoughts on Grades and Assessments During the Work Session

It is in the Work Session where grades and assessments are most likely to happen. The danger in having elements that are graded in other areas is that those assignments and their resulting grades can lean towards the compliance and completion nature of teaching rather than the progress and promise of learning. But for now, let's assume that in general most of the student work that will be graded or the majority of the assessments that will be given are housed here. With that said, here are just a few thoughts on the matter of grades we assign and the assessments we administer and how they do or do not relate to our purpose of designing learning.

Grades – At one time or another, many of us, veteran teachers, have had this at the back of our minds or have openly declared outright: grades are earned. I'm guilty of it. It took a few years for me to really look at my practices and profession to decide what grades really meant to my students and to me. We may have the mindset that grades are transactional, like a paycheck. You work and receive compensation. That practice is about compliance and may not really be about learning as we all along supposed.

So what do we do? Think about grades just like everything else we have designed for throughout this book. This leads us to a few questions: what is the purpose for this grade as it relates to learning? Does this grade promote feedback driving growth and learning? Will students know what this grade means to their learning? What will be the results of the grade as it relates to the next steps for students? In other words, what's in a number?

If grades, in the traditional sense, are something we will continue to use, how can we make the average in the grade book mean something to learning? First, let's not put anything into the grade book that isn't about learning. I remember wanting to miss a day of school here and there growing up. My parents' go-to was the thermometer, no fever meant I was going to school. There were times I was sly enough to be able to get that thermometer artificially heated up with a nearby light bulb. Typically I always sent it soaring too high; a temp of 122 would not be realistic. Still, there were times I managed to manipulate the mercury and stay home. I'm certain my parents knew the truth. How does this translate to the grade book? Anything we put in the grade book that is not about learning (notebook checks, homework completion checks, compliance-based grades) are just like that light bulb's effect on the thermometer. Something artificial has made an impact on the results. Think about what we are grading before it ever makes it to the average in the grade book.

Next to consider is this, when it does make it to the grade book, is that it? When the student gets the grade at the top of the paper, end of story? What we need to consider is how the grade can be used for the purpose of learning. Do the students conduct an error analysis of some kind to see exactly where the error in their thinking or current understanding was *and* do we allow them to learn, correcting their thinking, along with a change in the initial grade? This brings the question of the nature and purpose of grading itself back to our thinking. All I really want us to think about in a nutshell is this: if we all agree that learning is the job, what role do we want our grades to play in that? Make those decisions. Make the expectations clear for all involved: students, parents, school. And make the grades about learning.

Assessments – There will always be times when we need to take a minute and find out where we are in the learning journey. Assessments are a part of that process. Now, we can argue that everything students complete that provides evidence is an assessment of some kind. I would agree. Students work on a Task resulting in evidence that both they and we assess to understand where they are in their learning. This informs us about what feedback to provide and lets students know where they are in relation to where they want to go in their learning. But, for this topic's purpose, let's relate assessments to what they are in the traditional sense, a test.

We live in an educational world of tests. Personally, I feel we take a lot less than we did when I came through school, and I have noted a great reduction in tests where I have served as an educator for the last 22 years. But, we still have them. And they mean something. It's our job to navigate the accountability aspect assessments bring, and use the information gained from them in ways meaningful for learning while also making sure we are preparing students for the task that is an assessment.

One thing we must do is create assessments with learning in mind. That means creating assessments resulting in quality and reliable information serving as feedback for me as the learning engineer of the classroom to use moving forward. Assessments designed in this way that give a clear and real picture of what students know can help inform me of my next step in designing learning for them. Some of that is affected by the types of questions and number of questions we place on an assessment.

When I turned 15, I spent a year driving my parents' Chevy sedan around, with them in the car, of course. I learned how to operate the lights and turn signals. I practiced parallel parking and three-point turns. I got comfortable with the driving process and eventually went to take my driver's test the day I turned 16. If I had shown up to the test and the evaluator at the DMV asked me to get into a 1958 Ford Pickup with standard transmission in the steering column, I would not have walked away with my license that day. I had practiced and prepared in a completely different way than the test required. My parents are grateful that was not the case because I am sure they were ready to be freed from taking me around.

This reminds me of what we ask of students on our own assessments. Do ours in our class look and feel like "the one" they will be required to take later? You know "the one" I am referring to. It is the high-stakes, state-assigned assessment used to hold schools accountable. Until things change, that's how it is. So, if we only give fill-in-the-blank or true-and-false questions on our assessments in class, how will students know how to navigate "the one" later? If our tests in the room are only ten questions every time, what happens to our students when they face one that's 30 questions? Here's one for my fellow ELA folks that I was guilty of: if students are given three days in class to write a coherent essay, what happens when they face the same task on an assessment with a time limit of 90 minutes? Am I asking for more testing? Absolutely not. But we do need to ask if we are doing ourselves and our students a disservice by not, at the very least, preparing them for assessments later on through our own classroom-assessment uses.

Chapter 6 – The Instruction: Success Criteria, Tools, and Pathway Templates

Developing Success Criteria, Tools, and Pathways to introduce to students during the Instruction is a little like the work you did previously when digging into the standards to discover Learning Targets. We are making intentional, instructional choices based on what our students will need to complete the upcoming Task in the Work Session. This is a Task we have designed with engagement and challenge in mind that will show everyone in the room the evidence of learning required to meet the standard of the target we've set. Now, we have to decide what to look for in the evidence students are bringing to us that represents the qualities necessary to demonstrate the Learning Target was met. Defining these qualities will allow for the creation of a baseline of performance on the Task that shows what meeting the target looks like. We can also list some common qualities of work that typically fall short of the intended goal of the target. These can assist us in thinking of ways to proactively intervene with Tools targeting these areas. Utilizing the template in Table 8.7 can help you, together with a PLC team if possible for more input, dig into the Task to design criteria and tools we need to share during the Instruction.

TABLE 8.7 Success Criteria and Tools Development Template

Learning Target	
I can . . .	
The Task	
The students will . . . What is the Task that I am asking students to complete to show evidence they have met the Learning Target?	
Success Criteria Qualities	**Qualities Not Meeting the Target**
What observable qualities will the evidence of the Task have that show it meets the level of the Learning Target?	What misconceptions does the evidence of this Task have when it does not meet the Learning Target?
Possible Pathways	**Possible Tools**
How can we move students upward and deeper in their learning when they meet the Learning Target?	What possible tools can you provide for students to help eliminate some of the elements from the previous list?

Examples of Success Criteria

Below are some of the examples of Success Criteria I have found most effective for learning and beneficial for me as a teacher over the years. Each has its own purpose and place in the learning. What I would suggest as a litmus test for any Success Criteria you use is this: is what I am providing for my students as Success Criteria providing a clear picture of what their evidence will need to show in order to prove to themselves and to me they have indeed learned to the level of the target?

What that looks like might depend on the type of Task you have provided. It might depend on the type of information you are seeking from students concerning their learning relating to the Task. It might even depend on a process you are looking to improve relating to learning. Some of the most effective and engaging ones I have used have been when I have co-created the Success Criteria with students. It can be as simple as, "What do you think the qualities in our evidence of learning from today's Task should be to meet our learning goal?" Students sometimes come up with better stuff than I ever could. Plus, since they are the ones involved in the process of creating what success looks like, they are more likely to be agreeable and engaged since they were given a voice in the process. Whatever you use them for, in whatever format you choose, and by whomever they are created, make Success Criteria kid-friendly and meaningful to learning, and you won't go wrong. Use the following ideas to help give students the clarity they need to take ownership of their learning in your classroom.

Growth-Mindset Success Criteria

This one is my personal go-to for creating Success Criteria on my own or with students' input. The reason I like it so much is that it checks all the boxes for me in my design process. It allows students to see what should be visible in their own evidence. It allows me to design tools and pathways with specific purposes in mind. It also helps me focus any feedback discussions to what that next step should be.

In Table 8.8, I have included several examples of what these could look like at different grade levels and content areas. Feel

TABLE 8.8 Growth-Mindset Success-Criteria Examples

Learning Target: I can identify and classify types of figurative language.			
1	2	3	4
NO, I cannot identify or classify different examples of figurative language in a text YET.	YES, I can identify different examples of figurative language in a text, BUT I am having trouble classifying which type they are.	YES, I can identify and classify different examples of figurative language in a text by: 1. Finding an example of figurative language 2. Labeling the example as a simile, metaphor, hyperbole, personification, or idiom. 3. Writing examples of my own.	YES, I can identify and classify different types of figurative language in a text by: 1. Finding an example of figurative language 2. Labeling the example as a simile, metaphor, hyperbole, personification, or idiom. 3. Writing examples of my own. AND I can explain the effect these examples have on the text.
Learning Target: I can translate a geometric shape in a coordinate plane.			
1	2	3	4
NO, I cannot translate a geometric shape in a coordinate plane YET.	YES, I can attempt to translate a geometric shape in a coordinate plane, BUT I am having trouble with: – Identifying them – Notating them – Explaining my mathematical reasoning	YES, I can translate a geometric shape in a coordinate plane by producing: 1. A polygon drawn on a coordinate plane. 2. Translations drawn based on the notation. 3. Each translation is correctly labeled and explained. 4. My explanation uses my reason and mathematical evidence to support what I think.	YES, I can translate a geometric shape in a coordinate plane, 1. A polygon drawn on a coordinate plane. 2. Translations drawn based on the notation. 3. Each translation is correctly labeled and explained. 4. My explanation uses my reason and mathematical evidence to support what I think. AND I can make a Flipgrid video explaining the process to others.

TABLE 8.8 (Cont.)

Learning Target: I can explain why the physical characteristics of place affect where people choose to settle			
1	2	3	4
NO, I cannot explain why the physical characteristics of place affect where people choose to settle <u>YET</u>.	<u>YES,</u> I can identify the physical characteristics and human settlements <u>BUT</u> I cannot provide a reason for the settlements using the physical characteristics as evidence.	<u>YES,</u> I can explain why the physical characteristics of place affect where people choose to settle by: 1. Correctly identifying the physical characteristics of the region. 2. Correctly labeling the human settlements. 3. Providing a reason for why each settlement exists using the physical characteristics as supporting evidence.	<u>YES,</u> I can explain why the physical characteristics of a place affect where people choose to settle. by: 1. Correctly identifying the physical characteristics of the region. 2. Correctly labeling the human settlements. 3. Providing a reason for why each settlement exists using the physical characteristics as supporting evidence. <u>AND</u> I can explain how these settlements have affected the physical characteristics over time.

free to change up the labels to best meet your classroom culture. Keep in mind that we should design tools or pathways that provide guidance as students seek to move from one level to the next in their learning. If I have established the Learning Target and students have this Success Criteria to utilize along with tools and pathways, I can intensely intervene with a small group at level 1; students at level 2 have tools to access, and the rest have pathways to move beyond.

Single-Point Success Criteria

These are an easy, simple, and engaging way for students to self-assess at any moment in the learning process. Fluckiger (2010) completed a study on this specific type of student self-assessment and found that students were more engaged and helped each other more when using them. That's what we are designing for after all, right? Making them is simple. Start with the qualities that would meet the level of the standards-based learning target you have unwrapped and list the evidence you would expect to see in student work. Students then are free to self-assess at any stage of their work from the very beginning of the Task, right there in the middle of it, or even at the end when it has been completed. Learners are in a state of continual evaluation, reflection, and exploration as they consider what they know and have mastered related to the Task and what assistance or feedback they still feel in need of receiving as they move upward in their learning. This is exactly what we want out of our learners as they move through their learning utilizing examples similar to these in Table 8.9.

Continual Practices Success Criteria

There is no real estate more valuable in the classroom than the four walls surrounding your students, five if you throw the ceiling into the mix. I've been in classrooms at both ends of the spectrum. One with nothing but the minimum on the walls, like the fire drill routes or hall pass hanger. Another with every square inch of wall space covered that you would have to take things down to know the room's paint color. I am a huge proponent of making these walls work for you and your students. Many times that involves creating things to display instead of buying them. Decorate your room

TABLE 8.9 Single-Point Success-Criteria Examples

What I Know!	*Learning Target*	*What I Need!*
	I can solve two-step equations by . . . 1. Getting the variable alone on one side of the equal sign. 2. Using multiplication or division to figure out the value of the variable. 3. Checking the solution by substituting the value I found into the original equation.	
What I Know!	*Learning Target*	*What I Need!*
	I can write an engaging introductory paragraph for my essay that: 1. Uses an attention-getting method 2. Contains a clearly stated thesis of the whole essay 3. Joins the attention-getting method and the thesis using some type of connection method.	
What I Know!	*Learning Target*	*What I Need!*
	I can describe the difference between physical and chemical changes using: 1. A definition of each to show how they are different 2. A drawing or model created to compare them. 3. Observations from reactions to categorize their differences.	

however you see fit, but if we want the walls working for learning, we might have to take down a few kitten posters or motivational phrases to free up some space. Here's why. No matter what age or content you teach, chances are there are some common practices that you will want to work on or will be working in throughout the year. In an ELA class, it might be what a well-constructed paragraph or essay looks like. In math, examples of what math discussions or math talks need to exemplify. In science, what are the qualities that we should put in an effective analysis statement? In social studies, what does incorporating supporting evidence look like when we examine historical events?

Whatever subject you teach to whatever-age students, you can save yourself a lot of time while also handing responsibility back over to your students during their learning by creating (or having them create) quality Continual Practices Success Criteria. These can be in any format you wish or one that works best for your students. For example, your goal for the year is for students to write a quality paragraph with textual evidence included. You might have a series of student examples rated on a scale of 1–5 with the qualities of each identified underneath for students to compare. Students may start at a level 1 here in September, but the end goal for June at a level 5 is already available for reference during class.

Maybe you would want to utilize elements of the Growth Mindset example from above to create what qualities students need to be continually focused on during your math class all year long. You might want students' evidence of learning in math targeted with specific intention and attention on connecting conceptual knowledge and procedural practices. Create a criteria showing what this looks like or sounds like in math when learning and hold students to being able to understand it, use it, and grow from it. When using this type of Success Criteria, make locations known, your references to them purposeful, and the conversations surrounding their use as much a routine in your class as any other procedure. Whatever your method, the point behind them is having a model of what success looks like for these commonplace occurrences in your classroom available to and understood by students, so they can hold themselves and each other accountable to the evidence they will be providing for this practice.

Chapter 7 – The Closing: Examples

Additional Effective Strategies for the Closing

The Closing has a mission to serve in the learning, just as the Opening did. Again, do not feel pressured to be a master of them all; limit yourself to the ones that work most effectively in your classroom. We only need to keep the purposes of the Closing in mind when we are choosing our methods. The Closing has three main objectives: summarize the learning, reflect on the process, and praise both pitfalls and progress. In fact, many of the methods listed previously in the Opening-strategies list can be used for the Closing as long as those three purposes are the focus. Please try any method from Table 8.10 to design effective Closings for your lesson designs.

TABLE 8.10 Strategies for the Closing

Strategy	Method
Analogy Aloud	Students create an analogy comparing the learning of the day to something else, like a race, trip through the jungle, building a skyscraper, etc.
Blizzard	Students write down a list of things about the learning of the day, ball them up, and at the signal throw them up in the air. Students pick up a random "snowball" and read other students' responses.
Comic Strips	Students compose a comic strip illustrating the learning today in class.
Emoji Summary	Emojis are used as the primary mode of communication when recalling the learning of the day.
Fireworks and Feedback	Fireworks are the things that happened in learning today worthy of celebration, both successes and mistakes. Feedback are items students made use of from the teacher or peers that assisted them in moving learning forward. Students list these to share.
Foldable	Students construct a foldable to organize the information you would like to gain from the Closing.
Frayer Model	Students complete a Frayer model summarizing the learning of the day along with any additional information regarding reflection and revision of learning.
Head, Shoulders, Knees, Toes	Students point to these body parts and share the following information aloud. Head = What I know, Shoulder = How I helped or was a shoulder for someone Knees = What I still need Toes = What will I do TOE-morrow to grow in this learning.
Give One, Get One	In reaction to the teacher's prompt in the Closing, students produce a response, give it to another student and receive one from a fellow student, sharing, comparing, and contrasting their ideas.
Graffiti Wall	Place a big sheet of paper on a wall. Students write their responses as they relate to the Closing as words or images in graffiti-style art.
Once Upon a Time . . .	Students compose a retelling of the account of today's learning in the form of a fairy tale including all the typical aspects of a good story.

TABLE 8.10 (Cont.)

Strategy	Method
Stop/ Collaborate/ Listen	In the Closing, students stop to respond to a prompt, collaborate with others to share ideas, and are not responsible for sharing out their individual ideas, but rather the ideas of others as a result of their listening.
This One Thing	Students respond to the learning of the day with a single word. They share their word with others in the room and explain why this word best summarizes everything that happened today.
What? So What? Now What?	Students' responses in the Closing center around these three questions: what? – What did we learn? So What? – Why is it important? Now What? – Based on what happened in learning today, where will we need to go next?
WIG and WIN	What I Got and What I Need. Students list these in relation to the Learning Target of the day. Got = Things they are confident and have mastery over. Need = Things they are still unsure about or need more practice in relating to the learning.

Example Lesson Designs by Grade Levels

The following Lesson Design Template in Table 8.11 will assist in guiding you through the general design processes using many of the questions we addressed throughout the book. Here are several examples of Lesson Designs at different grade levels and various content areas as well. Personally, I tend to make these digital and link all of the items, resources, texts, tools, or anything else I will need to use for the lesson. However you choose to record your designs, I urge you to do so in a way that is meaningful and easy for you to access. I'm afraid there are places that have made the "Lesson Plan" so convoluted, complicated, and compulsory that the point of the plan has been lost altogether. Do we need to design? Yes, absolutely. But it needs to be a design that serves both learning and teacher use above all else.

TABLE 8.11 Lesson Design Template, Also Known as a "Lesson Plan"

Learning Target		I can . . . What's the Learning Target?
10%	The Opening	What method will be used to engage student curiosity and activate prior knowledge about the Learning Target?
25%	The Instruction	The Instruction provides the teacher Guided Information, Skills, and Tools needed to complete the Task in the Work Session.
What do students need to KNOW before starting the <u>task</u>?		Reading materials, notes, definitions, etc.
What do students need to be able to know how to DO before starting the task?		Processes to model, procedures, steps, etc.
Success Criteria The QUALITIES the <u>PRODUCT</u> must have to meet target		What CONCRETE and OBSERVABLE qualities does the product of the task have that SHOWS the student as well as the teacher that the learning target was indeed met?
Tools to Escape What do students need to move themselves upward in their learning to be proficient in this task?		These can be worked examples, student partners, answer sheets, anchor charts, process videos, the choices are endless.
Pathways to Accelerate What do students need to grow beyond proficiency?		Provide an avenue for students to move beyond just meeting the target. Move to accelerate or enrich the task.
50%	**The Work Session** A <u>Task</u> resulting in a <u>PRODUCT</u> that SHOWS the target was met	What will students be asked to do that results in a product demonstrating the meeting of the target?
15%	**The Closing**	What method will be used to summarize the learning of the day as it relates to the Learning Target?

Elementary Fifth-Grade ELA

This example design in Table 8.12 centers on the identification and classification of figurative language in a text. The opening Sort activity is composed of 16 different examples (4 of each type) of figurative language. Students are asked to sort these 16 examples into 4 different groups, no other instructions. The sort activity then moves into the discussion of the characteristics for the grouping. This leads into the Instruction, in which the class is informed of the four types. They can use the characteristics to construct definitions for the classifications.

The Work Session involves reading a short story, annotating for figurative language. Students record their findings and classify the type. Those at level 1 are in a small group with the teacher. A flowchart is provided as a tool to aid in classification for students at level 2. Students who are moving upward in their learning to level 4 may also extend their thinking about figurative language by using a pathway that guides them to composing an author's-purpose statement as it relates to the use and function of the examples they discovered.

The Closing is a This One Thing summarizer. Students must think of one word encompassing the learning of today. They relate that one word to their work in figurative-language identification, classification, and usage. They connect the success and struggle to this word as well in their responses.

TABLE 8.12 Fifth-Grade ELA "Figuring Out Figurative Language"

Learning Target		I can identify and classify examples of figurative language in a text.			
10%	The Opening	Sort – Using examples of metaphors, similes, hyperboles and personifications			
25%	The Instruction				
	KNOW	Short Story "Eleven" by Sandra Cisneros Figurative-language vocabulary with examples			
	DO	• How to annotate the text for examples • Identify the example and determine the type of language it is • Write examples of their own • Extending knowledge – how to use this information to explain author's purpose			
Success Criteria		**1**	**2**	**3**	**4**
		NO, I cannot identify or classify different examples of figurative language in a text YET.	YES, I can identify different examples of figurative language in a text, BUT I am having trouble classifying which type they are.	YES, I can identify and classify different examples of figurative language in a text by: 1. Finding an example of figurative language 2. Labeling the example as a simile, metaphor, hyperbole, personification, or idiom. 3. Writing examples of my own.	YES, I can identify and classify different types of figurative language in a text by: 1. Finding an example of figurative language 2. Labeling the example as a simile, metaphor, hyperbole, personification, or idiom. 3. Writing examples of my own. AND I can explain the effect these examples have on the text.

TABLE 8.12 (Cont.)

Tools to Escape		Figurative-language flowchart
Pathways to Accelerate		Writing-an-author's-purpose-statement guidance
50%	The Work Session	Students will annotate a text identifying figurative language and classifying the examples. Students will also compose five examples around a memory they have of an event. Level 4 will also contain author's-purpose statements constructed using the provided guidance.
15%	The Closing	This One Thing closing

Elementary/Middle Math

Table 8.13 summarizes a design that could be used in elementary or middle math classrooms depending on how simple or complex you want to make it. The premise is that the students have been hired by the local recreational-sports board to design a new sports complex for your city. The complex must include a space for a softball field, baseball field, soccer field, football field, as well as a centrally located concession stand and restrooms. The Draw It opening asks students to draw what they know about each type of field in regards to its size, shape, and other qualities.

The Instruction centers on giving the students the dimensions of their overall sports complex. The rest can be completed in multiple ways. The students can be given all of the dimensions to calculate the areas of each field and element. You can exclude some for students to have to use reasoning to determine. There is no limit to how you can modify this assignment for your learners. The Success Criteria can be co-created with students once they know the overall goal. Simply, make a list of all the qualities the class brainstorms together that would need to be included as evidence of quality learning.

The Work Session has the students using lined graph paper to draw out and label their sports-complex areas. Students needing tools can access anchor charts and Flipgrid videos prepared in earlier classes. Those students wanting to take learning deeper can add additional elements or shapes representing other structures at the complex and determine their area as well. Again, modifying this to meet where your students currently are or in order to make it more challenging is up to you.

The Closing is a Gallery Walk displaying each sports-complex plan from class. Students write down feedback for each as they walk around. Feedback is in the form of two stars and a wonder with the stars representing the things students liked about each design and the wonder asking a question they wonder about the design.

TABLE 8.13 "Recreational-Complex Planner"

Learning Target		I can determine the area of squares and rectangles (or other polygons)
10%	The Opening	Draw It
25%	The Instruction	
	KNOW	Procedural knowledge of determining area of targeted polygons.
	DO	Use procedural knowledge to determine the area with given values. Apply the same knowledge to determine areas with missing values. Draw shapes on lined graph paper.
Success Criteria		Co-created Success Criteria with student input.
Tools to Escape		Anchor charts and Flipgrid videos Small-group conferencing
Pathways to Accelerate		Students can add additional optional structures to their complex. Students can also be challenged with alternative predetermined values.
50%	The Work Session	Students work collaboratively or individually to plan their recreational complex using the given requirements. The products will have drawings, labeled dimensions, and calculated values.
15%	The Closing	Gallery Walk

Middle School Life Science

The example design in Table 8.14 focuses on the different systems in the human body and how they interact with one another to support life. The Opening is a simple turn and talk about leadership since the Task will require them to run an election campaign for the Leader of the Body elections.

The Instruction will mainly focus on the format and tools available for the Task. The students and their products will actually result in a Jigsaw that will inform students of each of the body's separate functions and interactions with each other. There are examples and criteria available for each element of the Task.

The Work Session involves the students choosing one of three minor campaign products (poster, buttons, or slogan) and one of three major campaign products (speech, presentation, campaign ad). Students have examples to reference. Their products must focus on three goals: communicating their body system's function, detailing how it interacts with all the other systems, and why their assigned system is the best choice to lead the whole human body. When completed, the students will present their minor and major campaign products to the rest of the class. Students record information in a graphic organizer.

The Closing is a Mock Election via a Google Form that not only collects votes, but also collects the justified reasons behind each of the votes based on the information learned in class about the human body systems' interactions with each other.

TABLE 8.14 Middle Grades Life Science "Body Systems Election"

Learning Target		I can explain how each system of the human body interacts with the others to support life.	
10%	The Opening	Turn and Talk – What makes an effective leader? What are the characteristics you look for?	
25%	The Instruction		
	KNOW	Functions of the seven main systems of the human body. How each system interacts with the others to keep humans alive. What are the general formats of political campaign components such as posters, buttons, speeches, and advertisements.	
	DO	Create their chosen products (poster, ads, presentations, etc.) Verbally present their campaign Record necessary information about body systems.	
Success Criteria	WIK	Body Systems I can explain how each system of the human body interacts with the others to support life by: 1. Analyzing and detailing the functions of my assigned system. 2. Analyzing and detailing how my system interacts with each one. 3. My explanations include how my system and its interactions are necessary for life.	WIN
	WIK	Campaign Elements 1. I include one minor and one major campaign element. 2. My elements include reasoning for my system to be chosen as leader of the body. 3. My reasons are supported with the evidence I have learned about my system.	WIN

TABLE 8.14 (Cont.)

Tools to Escape		Examples of campaign components with labels and information. Videos referencing body-system information. Graphic Organizer Campaign Components Doc YouTube Playlist
Pathways to Accelerate		Additional option: Writing a Political Debate between Systems.
50%	The Work Session	Students are campaign workers seeking to get their randomly assigned human body system elected as the "leader of the body." Students are given choices of three minor campaign elements and three major elements. Students complete one minor and one major and present information to class serving as a Jigsaw for instruction. Students collect information about other systems using a graphic organizer.
15%	The Closing	Mock Election via Google Form

High School US History American Revolution

The example design in Table 8.15 focuses on the different systems in the human body and how they interact with one another to support life. The Opening is a List It asking students to list the causes of relationship breakups. This discussion eventually will tie to the greatest breakup in American history, the American Revolution.

The Instruction centers on the previewing of the menu. Each section has a choice of items the students can consider completing as their tasks in their collaborative groups. Students are made aware of the location and operations of the different levels of reading materials as well as the other tools that will assist those who need guidance in finding information they need or in constructing quality analysis or evaluative statements.

The Work Session has students choose one item from the Appetizer (Colonial Period ideologies), Soup and Salad (Societal Situations), Main Course (major military engagements), and Dessert (Diplomacy and Declaration of Independence). Each section has three choices of items representing different mini-tasks that result in student evidence. Each evidence is evaluated with Success Criteria tailored to each menu section. Students access the Tools and the "Make it Spicy" add-on elements to navigate the assignment.

The Closing is a Graffiti Wall divided into the same sections of the menu. Students use images, words, much like Sketchnoting, to summarize their learning from each section. This wall will remain up for reference as students move forward into the events following the Revolution in order to see connections and draw conclusions from their previous learning.

TABLE 8.15 "Welcome to Cafe America"

Learning Target		I can analyze the key ideologies, military, social, and diplomatic aspects surrounding the American Revolution.
10%	The Opening	List It! What are the top five reasons for relationships breakups?
25%	The Instruction	
KNOW		Ideologies and philosophies related to the American Revolution. Key military battles during the Revolution. Societal movements, actions, and attitudes concerning the Revolution. Diplomatic relationships and alliances during the Revolutionary period.
DO		Research for necessary information. Explain the cause-and-effect relationship between historical events. Determining significance of historical events. Analyze the reasoning of historical events and decisions.
Success Criteria		Each menu section has a different set of requirements based on the choices. These are available on the menu as the "Nutritional Guides" for each item.
Tools to Escape		Articles and resources available on a variety of reading levels for students to access information. Students also have graphic organizers, sentence stems, and guiding questions for sections when they have difficulty targeting needed information.
Pathways to Accelerate		Students have a "Make it Spicy" option for each item they select off the menu. These options have additional elements students are asked to consider and incorporate into their menu tasks.
50%	The Work Session	Students work through the menu, choosing one item from each of the major sections.
15%	The Closing	Graffiti Wall

Closing Message

We have covered a lot of ground together in this book. What I want more than anything is for this to be a guiding resource as we all look to make what we do in the classroom more and more about learning and less about teaching. Chances are you are an already phenomenal teacher, otherwise you probably wouldn't have picked this book up in the first place, much less saw it through to the end. Thank you for who you are and what you continue to do for your kids every day. To all the educators making it here to the end and ready to make the shift from teaching to designing learning, I want to leave you with this one mission as you move forward: intention.

Do everything relating to learning with intention. This means making purposeful, meaningful decisions with the intended outcome already in your mind, and then look for the impact of your actions afterwards. Be intentional in everything you do. Be intentional in your actions and attitudes as you build relationships with your students. That may mean setting your intentions on "that one kid" and making connecting with that student a purposeful priority. Be intentional with engaging students' curiosity. Choose with their interests, context, and connections in mind. Be intentional with the methods of instruction you provided. Your attention to detail in the clarity you give means all the difference and can transform your classroom academically and behaviorally. Be intentional with the "work" you choose for your students to complete. Make the tasks given engaging, relevant, challenging, and something they will have to think through instead of just work through. Be intentional with how you choose to wrap learning up. Praise the progress, the mistakes, the struggle, and the successes. Be intentional in all things. After all, that's what a design is. A plan with a specific end in mind.

Remember, learning IS the job. We can teach like we always have, cross our fingers, and hope that it happens by default. Or, we can make the intentional choices required with the desired impact and end results in mind, giving learning a better chance of happening by design.

Reference List

Antonetti, J. V., & Garver, J. R. (2015). *17,000 classroom visits can't be wrong: Strategies that engage students, promote active learning, and boost achievement*. ASCD.

Corwin. (2021, August). *Visible learning Meta^x*. Retrieved September 7, 2022, from www.visiblelearningmetax.com/

Fluckiger, J. (2010). Single point rubric: A tool for responsible student self-assessment. *The Delta Kappa Gamma Bulletin, 76*(4), 18.

Hattie, J., & Clarke, S. (2018). *Visible learning: Feedback*. Taylor & Francis.

McKibben, S. (2014, July 15). *Two minutes to better student behavior*. ASCD. https://www.ascd.org/blogs/two-minutes-to-better-student-behavior

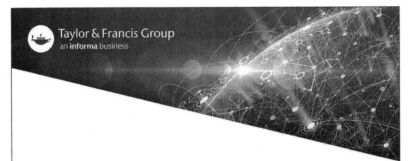

Made in the USA
Monee, IL
06 July 2023

38736247R00103